From the First Bite

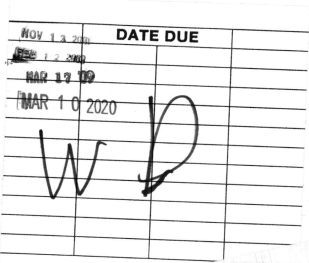

From the First Bite

A Complete Guide to Recovery from Food Addiction

Kay Sheppard, M.A.

Health Communications, Inc.
Deerfield Beach, Florida

www.hci-online.com

Library of Congress Cataloguing-in-Publication Data

Sheppard, Kay

From the first bite: a complete guide to recovery from food
addiction / Kay Sheppard.

  p. cm.

Includes bibliographical references.

ISBN 1-55874-754-0 (trade paper)

1. Compulsive eating. 2. Twelve-step programs. I. Title: Food
addiction 2. II. Title: From the first bite. III. title.

RC552.C65 S42 2000

616.85'26–dc21

00-056699

Publisher: Health Communications, Inc.
        3201 S.W. 15th Street
        Deerfield Beach, FL 33442-8190

Cover design by Larissa Hise Henoch
Inside book design by Dawn Grove

*In loving memory of
Stuart Brown,
recovery was the desire of his heart;
and Charlott Chaplin,
who was the dearest of friends.*

Contents

Foreword

Fresh out of medical school and in the throes of my internship, I landed my first job as a doctor: assistant medical director to the Compulsive Overeating Recovery Program. Sure, it sounds like a fancy title, but in reality, I was nothing more than an apprentice. I'd co-sign charts, write a few prescriptions and perform the obligatory health check with my stethoscope. But mainly my job was to stay out of the way and let the therapists do the "real" work.

I can't say that I blame management for keeping me in a low-profile, stealth mode. At the time, I had never even heard of food addiction. Consequently, the chances of me making any sort of therapeutic impact were slim to none. So in silence, I observed . . . and I began to witness miracle after miracle unfold. Men and women, young and old, who struggled with compulsive overeating for their entire lives, found long-lasting recovery. It was amazing! Needless to say, I wanted to be a more integral part of their healing. So I asked the lead therapist, "What's the best way to understand the origins, treatment and recovery process of compulsive overeaters?" Her answer was short and sweet: "Kay Sheppard." And she handed me Kay's first book, *Food Addiction: The Body Knows*. It changed my life.

Food addiction: The body knows. How very true. But all too often, family, friends, doctors and maybe even you refuse to listen. Yet your cravings are undeniable. Your binges are irrefutable. Your obsessions are a constant reminder that compulsive overeating is not a matter of weakness or willpower. Food addiction is a true disease.

The connections between mood, food and body chemistry are supported by countless studies. Many note a striking similarity to the underlying physiology of alcoholism. (After all, what's alcohol but liquid sugar with a kick?) Other studies reveal a powerful correlation between compulsive overeating and the brain chemistry of mood and anxiety disorders. Still others focus on the psychological powers that food possesses to either simulate or squelch various emotional states. To fully understand the impact and meaning of these studies, you can either spend the next decade living in a library, attending medical school, then specializing in addictionology and eating disorders, as I have done; or you can simply sit back, relax and begin to listen to yourself. After all, the body knows . . . and so does Kay Sheppard!

Kay Sheppard is the leading authority on helping others overcome compulsive eating. Her writings are required reading within the treatment community. As a successful author, Kay has a talent for taking the complex interplay between mind and body and making it both understandable and meaningful. As an accomplished clinician, Kay has a unique ability to empathize and touch each reader on a personal level. But the beauty of Kay goes beyond her expertise at prose and empathy. It is her gift of truly understanding the life and times of a food addict. For Kay herself has walked in the shackles of food addiction, but for decades now has found the freedom to walk the path of recovery. Join her. Enjoy *From the First Bite: A Complete Guide to Recovery from Food Addiction.*

Matthew S. Keene, M.D., is the founder and director of Feeding Your Feelings, a multi-disciplinary team of health-care professionals dedicated to the management of compulsive overeating through the development of human potential. He graduated with honors from Georgetown University School of Medicine and received his psychiatric residency training at the Cleveland Clinic Foundation. A national consultant, trainer and psychopharmacologist, Dr. Keene is the author of the award-winning book, *Chocolate Is My Kryptonite: Feeding Your Feelings: How to Survive the Forces of Food.*

Acknowledgments

Deep and lasting appreciation to generous and gracious friends Barbara Caravella, Jan Brown, Brenda Robinson, Gary Broyhill and John Whalen for your major contributions to this effort.

Gratitude to Lanie Reed, Ellen Dominguez, Pat Caron, Elaine Simon, Pete Meeker, Margot Escott, Dede Neufeld, Diane Fulton, Estelle Accalia and Richard and Penny Evans for your contributions, support and enduring friendship.

Many thanks for the thoughtful contributions from Matt Keene, M.D., Patrick Patrone, M.D., Carl Mashek, Diane Kamerzel, Danna Parkoff, Cynthia Kethley, Katy Kusk, Barbara Bird, Caren Glazer, Fran Shelton, Christine Hazelton, Dana Walling, Tebayane Dearth, Amie Taylor, Mert Rosenberg, Bari Bertoia, Yvonne Clark, Bradley Blankman, Patty Brooks, Judy Smith and Marisa Therrian.

To Alan W., Judy M., Judy Z., Robin S., Cynthia C. and Christine B., thanks for sharing the joys of recovery with us.

Gratitude to the folks at Health Communications, especially for the special efforts of Christine Belleris, Allison Janse and Kim Weiss. Boundless appreciation to Peter Vegso, Teri Peluso and Jackie Kozlowski for your many kindnesses and considerations over the past years. Much gratitude to Kathleen Fox, who did a terrific job creating order out of chaos. Thanks, Kathleen.

To all the food addicts who have taught me about this

addiction, especially Janet G., thank you from the bottom of my heart. Together we can do what we could never do alone.

Above all, prayerful thanks to the merciful God, who leads us out of addiction.

Introduction

A family member asks, "Where is the rest of that cake we had last night?" You react with panic. As your mind is creating an answer for your loved one, your gut is grinding with tension. You say, "The kids must have finished it," or "I gave it away," but you know the truth—that you ate it all. Shame, fear and anguish surface as you tell one more lie about your eating.

Millions of people have lost control over their consumption of food. Diets, fasts, pills, purging and weight-loss programs have become a way of life—all futile attempts to deal with this lack of control. Recent studies show that more than 50 percent of Americans are overweight and 22 percent are obese, despite weight-loss products and services costing thirty-three billion dollars a year. Over three hundred thousand people are dying per year from obesity. The shocking truth is that these studies do not even include those people whose bodies are at a normal weight or even underweight but who cannot control their eating. They are dying, too.

There is an answer! I found a way that works in 1967, and it has been working for me ever since. How I wish I could deliver those ideas on a silver platter! Since I cannot, I am offering this book packed with helpful information to support you in your efforts to overcome food addiction. That is what is on this silver platter—tools for recovery. These tools are meant for people new to the program, for others who have relapsed, and as ongoing support for those in successful recovery.

Certainly everyone has different ideas about what helps them on their recovery path. This particular path offers information about addiction, abstinence and a plan that works. It summarizes material I have collected since the publication of my earlier book, *Food Addiction: The Body Knows,* which tells "what the body knows" about the illness of food addiction from the physiological origins through physical stabilization in recovery. Since the publication of that first book, research conducted from Florida to California supports this work. One reader says, "The book taught me how I could get rid of the food that was controlling me and stop trying to control my food."

Now is the time to share new discoveries and insights in a new book by introducing up-to-date information and extending the scope to include physical, mental, emotional and spiritual recovery. We know there is scientific foundation for a food plan which eliminates all addictive substances, and the research continues to expand our knowledge.

Although I have had valuable feedback and information from nutritionists, researchers and professionals in the fields of addiction treatment, relapse prevention and research, most of the information I have gleaned over the years comes not from the professionals, but anecdotally from other recovering or relapsed food addicts. From this information, we have developed a program that works. It includes a revised food plan that eliminates cravings and stabilizes the body; practical ways to deal with mental, emotional and physiological triggers; a Twelve-Step guide; relapse prevention awareness; and a review of the barriers to a strong recovery. Consider this book to contain the best information we have today. There is no doubt that there will be more and better information tomorrow.

The Twelve Steps
of Alcoholics Anonymous

1. We admitted we were powerless over alcohol—that our lives had become unmanageable.
2. Came to believe that a Power greater than ourselves could restore us to sanity.
3. Made a decision to turn our will and our lives over to the care of God as we understood Him.
4. Made a searching and fearless moral inventory of ourselves.
5. Admitted to God, to ourselves and to another human being the exact nature of our wrongs.
6. Were entirely ready to have God remove all these defects of character.
7. Humbly asked Him to remove our shortcomings.
8. Made a list of all persons we had harmed, and became willing to make amends to them all.
9. Made direct amends to such people wherever possible, except when to do so would injure them or others.
10. Continued to take personal inventory and when we were wrong promptly admitted it.
11. Sought through prayer and meditation to improve our conscious contact with God as we understood Him, praying only for knowledge of His will for us and the power to carry that out.

12. Having had a spiritual awakening as the result of these steps, we tried to carry this message to alcoholics and to practice these principles in all our affairs.

AUTHOR'S NOTE

The quotations and personal stories used in this book are the actual experiences and thoughts of real people, used with their permission. With the exception of the author's story, the names have been changed or first names and initials are used in order to protect the confidentiality and anonymity of these individuals. In one history, the experiences of more than one person have been combined.

1

Three
Food Addicts
Tell Their
Stories

Kay's Story—The Author's Experience

Do you know you talk a lot about food and weight?" My recovery from active food addiction started with those words from a friend. Since I wasn't aware, I answered, "No, I didn't realize that." Then Janet asked another question: "Do you know there is a Twelve-Step program for that problem?" I didn't know that, either. She invited me to attend.

Well, it was November, and no food addict in her right mind would consider going into a recovery program before the holidays. No, indeed, I would wait until January to start anew. I was no dummy; I had lots of holiday eating to do! I don't recall the holiday festivities that year, but I do remember that I purchased a box of candy for my father for Christmas—then ate five of them before the gift got wrapped and delivered to him.

As I was walking from the bedroom, where I had hidden the fifth box of candy in my bottom dresser drawer, to the bathroom where I planned to eat it, I had a thought. *Why didn't I put this box of candy out on the coffee table and share it with my family?* That was my moment of truth. There was something very wrong with bedroom storage, bathroom eating. And I felt so selfish that I had not shared. This behavior was not new. Oh, no. I had spent my whole life buying treats for others and then secretly eating them all. Why, I was so good at hiding my eating that my husband commented, "I don't know why you have a weight problem, you eat like a bird."

My secret eating of sweets started at a fairly young age. As a small child, locked in the pantry to avoid detection, I would squeeze chocolate chips out of a tiny slit in the corner of the bag. Quietly opening the refrigerator, I would run my finger around the edge of the cake, collecting as much frosting as possible. All my nickels and dimes traveled to the corner store with me for sweet purchases. We had two corner stores, and when I got old enough to cross the street, I could get to the second one and buy ice cream cones dipped in chocolate sprinkles. What an innovation! When I found a dime at our vacation cottage, I talked my sister into rowing our boat miles to a concession stand to buy candy. I wonder if I shared with her.

Holidays were heaven! We got huge baskets filled with treats at Easter. We baked special family recipes at Christmastime. We decorated cakes for every occasion. I was obsessed with food. By the time I was in eighth grade, I was fat. We had to shop in the "chubby" clothes department. My mother dressed us beautifully, and she really had to search to find appropriate clothes for me. I started cooking about that time, too, making meals for the family. I just loved to be around food. By the time I was in high school, I was a talented pastry chef. I planned to be a dietitian when I grew up. I didn't really know what a dietitian was, but I figured it was about food and that would be great. I never did follow through on that idea.

At age fifteen, I went on my first diet and managed to lose twenty-two pounds by eliminating sweets and starches.

This was the first of many attempts to lose weight. Around that age I started smoking my dad's cigarettes. Within a few years, I started to drink alcohol. None of these addictive substances seemed to be out of control, but I had three of them operating: food, nicotine and alcohol. Everything appeared to be manageable. I had no idea about the progression of addiction; I was in the early stages and poly-addicted.

Alcohol was the first to become unmanageable. Not that I noticed. Denial took care of that. I was a binge drinker with a pattern of disruptive incidents followed by long periods of abstinence from alcohol. I would smoke and eat through the dry times as I got my life back together. My losses from alcohol mounted: my college education, a marriage, several jobs. By the time I found recovery, I had been institutionalized and separated from my young son.

In 1967, I got sober and began working a recovery program. My son and I were living with my parents. My mother asked me if I realized that I ate the whole pan of brownies every Sunday. It must have been noticeable that I was an automatic eater without awareness of my actions.

For the next ten years, I would rely on food and nicotine as my major addictive substances. During that time, my mother died of the complications of her own food addiction. She said to me the year before she died, "For the rest of my life I am going to eat the way I want to." She was surrendering to the disease. She told me that she had "given up." Mom died at age sixty-five. I had always been aware of her struggle with food. We began dieting together when I was fifteen. We tried lots of diets, drugs and programs. Nothing had worked for us.

In 1977 Janet introduced me to a recovery plan for compulsive eaters. I just loved it. Although I threw myself into the program, it would take several years in recovery before I realized the extremely serious nature of this disease. At first for me, it was mostly a weight-loss program and fellowship with people I really liked. My sponsor guided me for the first nine months of my recovery while I completed the first Three Steps. Then she got busy in graduate school, and I neglected to find a new sponsor. We moved to the country and I was no longer as connected with my recovering friends. Fewer meetings, fewer phone calls, one too many resentments, and I was back into the food—for one binge! That was enough to show me that I was as crazy on food as I had ever been on alcohol. It was time to get serious about recovery. I began to attend many meetings and moved forward in my Step work. It was no longer a weight-loss issue, it was a question of sanity.

After attending graduate school, I went to work as an addictions counselor in a treatment center where there was a food addiction unit. In the therapeutic community, the intense pain caused by food addiction was more apparent than in the meeting rooms. My eyes were further opened to the serious nature of this disease. I learned a lot about food plans and addictive foods there, too. Two years later, I went on to open several food addiction programs in hospital settings for another company. It was difficult to find support for abstinence in my new location. Because the major recovery program had stopped using food plans and effective guidelines for abstinence, members were not in stable physical recovery. It was frustrating, and sometimes I left meetings feeling defeated. Eventually, abstinence-based recovery took root in the community.

Over the years I collected a lot of information about food plans and addictive foods. Most of it came from recovering people. Many professionals offered good ideas, too. Developing an effective food plan has been a work in progress. Scientific research is catching up with us, but our best information comes from realizing what substances or situations trigger our craving. The body knows. What the body knows is this: It is sensitive to addictive substances and will always, without exception, react in an addictive manner to them. A great gift of recovery is relief from craving and obsession triggered by food substances.

In 1988 I quit smoking, and I spent the next two years suffering from acute and post-acute withdrawal. I relied on my sponsor and the God of my understanding to get through it. Others who had agonized during nicotine withdrawal assured me, "This too shall pass." I didn't believe it, but I didn't think they would lie, either. One day at a time, I did not pick up any addictive substances.

Nicotine was the last of my addictive substances. Without it, I had to watch my food carefully. I learned about discipline, obedience, commitment, vigilance and resolve. Alcohol, nicotine and caffeine were never in my home. However, I still had to prepare and eat food. Over the years the food processors introduced sugar and refined starches into foods that didn't need them. One food distributor told me there was a "conspiracy to get as much sugar as possible into food so that people would buy more." It became even more important to check labels. My recovery was strengthened. It was important to trust God, keep my side of the street clean, help others and work the steps. Food was a greater challenge than it had ever been before.

Today, I continue to weigh and measure my food, plan it daily and report it often to my sponsor. When attending a social event that includes eating, I eat beforehand, take my food with me or call ahead to arrange for abstinent food. Planning is the key to physical abstinence, and for that I am responsible. I do not just "show up" and expect others to have abstinent food waiting for me. For example, recently I did a workshop in south Florida. I took my food for the two meals I would need on the day of the program and spoke in advance with my host to arrange dinner for the evening before the workshop. I was served acceptable protein and starch but had to request another vegetable. The salad served contained cheese and bacon, neither of which is on my food plan. Assertive, not aggressive, requests usually result in great cooperation from servers, friends and relatives.

My relatives are familiar with my abstinence, and they are so cooperative. My sisters always have my kind of food available when I visit. My brother picks me up at the airport and pulls into the grocery store before we get to his home. "Get the food you need," he says. In restaurants I order dry, broiled protein, a dry baked potato, a large salad (no cheese, bacon, croutons) with oil and vinegar on the side, and water to drink. I don't use balsamic vinegar because it contains sugar. I don't use table salt because iodized salt contains sugar, too. When traveling I have all the food I will need on hand until I can get to a grocery store (every city, foreign or domestic, has one) or restaurant. I plan my travels meal by meal. I carry my scale and some condiments in my purse.

I seek objective feedback from my sponsor when I get into personality conflicts. I am willing to follow directions. Being openminded is so much easier than suffering. I have learned that whenever I judge, criticize, blame or put expectations on others, I become a helpless, hopeless, powerless victim of my own creation. I create my own pain, my own victimhood. When I want out of it, I do my work—which is to suspend judgment, give up expectations, stop blaming and get back to a place of love and acceptance. I call my sponsor occasionally, and I sponsor others. I attend meetings, usually daily. My goal is to do Steps Ten, Eleven and Twelve every day, always remembering the First Step—that I am powerless over certain foods. The literature is important to me.

In the morning I meditate, pray and read. In the evening I inventory, journal, resolve personality conflicts and do a gratitude list. When I am wrong I admit it, not always promptly, but it is always a relief when I do it. It takes so much energy and causes so much anguish to be "right." I understand the false idea that "I am right, you are wrong, you had better change!" causes all the fights, war and conflict in the world. By giving it up, I can resign from the conflict and enjoy peace. I would rather be happy than "right." In the world of the spirit there is no right/wrong, good/bad, could/should, only love and acceptance. That is where peace is found.

You can't keep it unless you give it away. Love and service are the recovery principles embodied in Step Twelve. I sponsor others, make phone calls, share at meetings and carry the key to the meeting room to ensure that the door will be open to every food addict seeking recovery. E-mail, chat rooms and our recovery loop provide opportunities to share on the Internet.

God's grace pours down upon me. All I have to do is say yes to all that he provides. He sent me countless people to help me; some told me about recovery, others taught me to meditate, still others showed me that I am the author of my own life. God's grace is always available to me, as I seek this day's reprieve from addiction. Coasting does not work. I cannot stay abstinent, clean and sober by putting anything before spiritual growth. Pain sends me scurrying for help. A very spiritual man taught me how to use pain as a spiritual path, but pain is not the only way to grow spiritually. The Twelve Steps show me how to bring my will into alignment with God's will. That is the direction in which I move. As my recovery progresses there is more of God, less of me. God is my home, and I have been moving homeward for years.

Malcolm's Story

He vividly describes the stages of food addiction, relapse and stable recovery. Obsessed with food, obsessed with weight, his struggle ended when he found a simple program that works!

I can remember being obsessed with food as far back as my memory goes. I had a good family; my three sisters and I were never abused, and we lived in what you would think was a perfect situation. My father had a good, secure job;

my mother stayed home to take care of us kids; we went to church; there were no drugs or alcohol in our house.

But at an early age I remember feeling frightened and lonely a lot of the time. I was shy and had trouble relating to people. I found comfort from these painful and confusing emotions in food. Our family diet was rich in sugar and refined carbohydrates, with big meals, plenty of snacks and a lot of high-fat Southern cooking. The earliest binge I can remember was about the age of four or five. By the time I started school, a lot of my eating patterns were already set. I had reached the point where I would get anxious if I thought I couldn't get binge food. It was a relief to find out they served vanilla wafers and Kool-Aid at kindergarten every morning!

I soon became seriously overweight and got my first taste of the taunts that all fat children suffer. I was sensitive and very shy, so these words really hurt and drove me further inside myself. My first diet was in the fourth grade and included amphetamines prescribed by the family doctor. I lost a little weight but promptly gained it back, starting a pattern that would be with me for years to come.

In elementary school I had to shop for clothes in the "husky" section and came to hate that word. I also hated the many reminders that I was different—not fitting in certain chairs or children's rides at the fair, getting out of breath easily, and comments about my weight from friends, relatives and other children. The more I was reminded of my inadequacies, the more I ate.

I was usually at the head of my class in academics and was talented in music and art. This was a mixed blessing; it gave me some self-esteem and helped keep me going, but it also gave some of the kids in my classes one more reason to hate me: the smart, fat kid who was the teacher's pet.

As I approached adolescence, I found out the main detriment to being a fat kid: The girls didn't like fat boys. Again I withdrew, and I ate. By eighth grade I weighed over two hundred pounds and was the second-biggest kid in school. Some of the other fat kids seemed so assertive and confident, while I was ashamed, guilty and afraid. Feeling different even from other fat kids really set me apart.

In high school I got involved in a popular rock and roll band, which really boosted my self-esteem for a while. I lost weight, grew my hair long and started wearing "cool" clothes and hanging out with older students who were into rock and roll and being hip. Despite all this, I could never seem to get over my fear of girls. I may have lost some weight, but I was still a fat kid on the inside. I did well in high school for my first two years, then in grade eleven I discovered alcohol and drugs. By age seventeen I was doing cocaine, speed and LSD, and I was arrested for possession of marijuana, which was a devastating blow to my parents and which got me off drugs temporarily. My food seemed to take second seat to the dope and booze at this time, though I was still overweight and my eating habits hadn't changed.

In college I soon slipped back into drug and alcohol use. As the months passed, I lost interest in my studies and was more interested in drugs and alcohol. Along with that, bad eating habits continued: quick food, snacks, no real meals, midnight pizza runs and trips to the all-night 7-Eleven for junk food. I began to put on weight again, rapidly.

By my third year I was increasingly isolated with my drugs and my food, I weighed three hundred fifteen pounds and was on the verge of flunking out. I was still terrified of girls, so I would go to food and drugs for affection. About this time I joined my first diet club, lost some weight and made an attempt to succeed in my classes. This lasted for a while, but eventually I went off the diet, my drug use increased again and I went through periods of depression.

After over six years in college I was still a junior. I was offered an opportunity to move to Washington, D.C., and I jumped at the chance for a fresh start. My family was so confused and weary of me by this point that they hoped the new job would help.

My first year in Washington was very exciting, but hardly a fresh start. I met lots of people who didn't seem to notice how fat I was or care about my drug abuse. I had very meager jobs, but it was all I needed to pay rent, buy food and get drugs. When I got really low, I would call home to Mom and Dad, making up a story about my car being in the shop. I began shoplifting to supply my food, which left more money for drugs. I became addicted to speed and other narcotics and eventually moved into a place in the middle of the worst part of the city. My diet grew worse: mostly fried food and pizza coupled with large amounts of pastry, crackers, candy, cake, ice cream and cookies. My roommates would watch in amazement as I ate an entire bag of chocolate chip cookies every day. Many bad incidents involving drugs happened during this time. That, coupled with my food binges, put me in an extremely bad mental, emotional and physical condition. I was barely able to hold down a job at this point due to constantly calling in sick, coming in late and never putting in a good day's work when I did show up. While at work, I was obsessed with eating out of vending machines and often would find ways to sneak to the snack bar. I knew deep down that something was wrong. I erroneously believed that if I could just lose weight, I would be okay. There was still no romantic involvement. Food and drugs were my lovers.

About this time in 1984, some friends of mine began a self-improvement program and they convinced me to try it, too. The application form asked what I wanted to accomplish with the program. I wrote, "Stop doing drugs, lose weight and get a girlfriend." So I was at least asking for help in a way. The therapy program had a profoundly positive influence on me. Over the two weekends that I was there, something happened. To this day, I don't know what caused it, but I woke up. I stopped doing drugs, joined a health club and went to a diet program. I got a better job at a very highly regarded company, where I would stay for nine years. Within a year I had dropped one hundred twenty pounds and was getting in really good physical shape at the gym. I had no spiritual program. I pretty much considered myself an agnostic, "borderline" atheist. This particular program was sectarian, which I liked a lot. I found a girlfriend at this time, a lady who had also done the program. She was a bulimic who had stopped purging. We fell in love and were married several years later.

Life was better: I eventually reached my goal weight of one hundred sixty-five pounds. I realize now that was way too thin for me. I shocked a lot of people with my transformation.

I was off drugs and only occasionally drank a little beer or wine. My job was going great. I was engaged to be married. I was happy, at least on the surface. Underneath, I was still scared. Although no longer the shy person of my youth, I still lived in a lot of fear of people. I was obsessed with staying thin. I would weigh myself four or five times a day. If my weight went up one pound, I would fast until the magic number again appeared on the display.

My fiancée and I went to the beach that summer for a vacation and had a huge argument. We didn't speak for the entire eight-hour drive home. When I got to the house, I ate an entire pie that we'd bought at the beach. It was my first binge since losing weight and was far more ferocious than anything I'd ever done before. I spent the next couple of days fluctuating between bingeing and fasting. I was still obsessed with my weight, and this was terrifying to me. I had drifted away from the therapy program by now and was out there on my own. The one thing the program had offered was a support system, but without it I didn't stand a chance. It wasn't long before the urge to use drugs returned. I went on a couple of weekend benders, which terrified my fiancée. I would disappear for a couple of days, then call her, apologize and then go home and go back to life as usual.

The problem was that I was almost thirty years old and had never dealt with childhood fears, plus I did not know I was a food and drug addict. As far as I was concerned, I had licked all those problems. After a brief breakup over the drugs, my fiancée and I got back together with the stipulation that I would seek counseling. I went to the counselor with a lot of apprehension. This was my first one-on-one experience with a mental health professional and I did not know what to expect. I wrote out my life story on an evaluation sheet for her and she read it. We began to talk and she suddenly said, "I think you should check out some of the Twelve-Step groups. They might be really good for you." She gave me meeting schedules for OA (Overeaters Anonymous), AA and NA (Narcotics Anonymous) and asked me to go to one meeting of each and report back. I don't know why, but I did not seem threatened by that suggestion at all. I didn't really plan to start going, but it seemed interesting. I had already done some therapy, so it seemed familiar to go to a "self-help" setting.

I don't remember those first meetings well, but I knew I needed to be there. I started going to NA almost immediately. I mainly listened the first few months. I liked the people. Their experiences were like mine. Some of them had been in recovery a long time. That was impressive! I started going to AA, which is where I really learned about the Steps. I had no sponsor and really didn't know anyone in the rooms, but I liked attending. I went to three to four meetings a week for several months. I didn't go back to OA, thinking I could handle the food on my own by working out and going to a diet club. By Christmas, I was back in the binge cycle again: five days of dieting, followed by two days of bingeing, followed by a one-day fast. It was driving me crazy and it was frightening. I couldn't stop bingeing and I knew it.

In January of 1987 I went back to OA for the second time. This time I stayed. I got a sponsor, and after six weeks I realized I had not binged once. I was at a normal weight at this time, about one hundred eighty-five pounds, so some people wondered what I was doing in OA. But as I shared my story they realized I belonged. I was taken care of by all the women in the OA program. They were very accepting of me. I learned so much about the steps from them. There were about fifteen women for every man in the Washington area. Those women really worked the program and carried the message, and they kept me abstinent.

Of course, when I say abstinent, I mean abstinent from bingeing and overeating, because that's all I knew at the time. There were no food plans in OA at that time, so I went on a plan of three meals a day with nothing in between. I abstained from sugar as part of my abstinence. I was still on wheat, but did not binge, so I didn't care. After three years in OA I had maintained my weight and worked through the Steps with my sponsor. I had also found a Higher Power, possibly for the first time in my life. I was not going to church or anything like that, but I had cracked open that door to God. I didn't like talking about it, though; I was still too much of an intellectual to start gushing about a Higher Power. My spirituality was very quiet and very personal, but it was there. I continued to work with my sponsor and also sponsored people myself. My recovery community was a huge part of my life. I still stay in touch with some of the people that I met at those first meetings.

I had several sponsors and they all helped me. My second was a food sponsor. It was the first time I had ever reported my food plan to anyone. I didn't want anyone to know what I ate! It was like a big secret. Nobody in meetings ever talked about food, so I didn't know what anyone ate and I was afraid that I was doing it wrong. I remember the first time I went out to eat with OA people. It was really stressful and weird. After a few times I got used to it, but in the beginning I found it a very uncomfortable experience. My food sponsor helped, although he was kind of gruff and I didn't look forward to talking to him. Because of this, I eventually stopped calling him. I guess I just didn't have the willingness to let go of my food at that point. Even though in my mind and heart I was abstinent, I still had some doubts.

After a few years, I completed the first Eleven Steps. I did service and enjoyed it. I went to many meetings, but I had started adding some questionable items back into my food plan. I had decided that "sugar-free, fat-free" frozen yogurt was all right, so I had a cup every night. I became obsessed with that frozen yogurt. If I was in some situation where I couldn't get it, I would get almost in a panic. My parents visited me one weekend and we went out to eat. On the way back to their hotel, I said, "I need to stop and get some frozen yogurt somewhere." Well, it was late and nothing was open, so we kept driving from one place to another trying to find it. We must have spent thirty or forty minutes driving around looking for a grocery store so I could get my fix. I didn't have a clue that I was addicted!

I began drifting away from NA but stayed in OA. About this time I started doing meditation and yoga with a local teacher and decided that this was a higher form of recovery than the Twelve Steps. I began to feel that it was time to leave them behind and get enlightened. I began studying Buddhism and meditating daily. My teacher was an amazing person, but she was also not an addict and didn't understand my real needs. I was not going to any OA, AA or NA by this time and had stopped calling my sponsor. My relationship with wife had suddenly gone sour, too. We stopped communicating and before I knew it, we separated and eventually divorced. It happened so fast that I always wonder why we didn't even bother trying to save the marriage.

By early 1992 I was divorced and facing the world as a single man again. I was terrified. Even though I had been married, I still felt uncomfortable about women. Looking back on it, I think I married my wife because I thought I'd never get another woman. I did end up with a girlfriend, though, one who didn't drug or abuse food, so she was a safe person for me. I remember being ashamed to tell her that I had not had any alcohol in six years, because I didn't want her to think I was some kind of straight-arrow loser. My abstinence was shaky, and about halfway though the year I started bingeing. For the first time in many years, I was in an uncontrollable state with food. Midnight trips to the convenience store were followed by sugar hangovers and much fear and self-hatred.

At the end of the year I was offered a chance to become a professional musician, something I had always dreamed of. So in January 1993 I resigned my job of nine years and went off on the road with a rock and roll band. I threw my program and spirituality out the window and went on the wildest ride of my life. The next two years of touring were exhilarating, frustrating, exciting and painful, all in one. I felt like a rock star. I had started drinking again about six months into the band tour. The other guys all smoked pot and drank beer, and that looked pretty good to me after seven years clean. So I thought a little beer wouldn't hurt. This lifestyle was so consuming that I totally stopped working on myself as a person and just became a character in the group. I wanted to be rich and famous. We were hanging out with people who were. In 1994 the band's popularity started slowing down. Our CDs didn't sell well and the money stopped coming in. We eventually lost our record contract, and by September 1994 it was all over.

I was in such denial about the band breaking up that I kept waiting for the phone to ring with an offer to join another band. But the offers never came. So I ate and started putting on weight again. I went to a few OA meeting during this time, only to find out that I was kind of a legend: someone who had gone out into the world and "made it." So I could not admit the truth to anyone. I never could get back into the groove of going to meetings. I was working for temporary agencies to pay rent and continued using drugs and alcohol. After a terrible two-month fling with a woman who was an abusive alcoholic, I returned to my drugs with a vengeance. I used like never before. I ate whatever I wanted and whenever I wanted. I became suicidal and honestly did not expect to live to see the end of the year. I had no program, no God in my life and no hope.

In May of 1995 I checked myself into a detox program and got off drugs. I went to my first NA meeting in years, where I was welcomed. I moved back to North Carolina and eventually settled down and picked up a white chip in August of 1995. (A white chip is a poker-shaped chip, which is distributed in some groups to newcomers or those who have returned after a relapse. The chip represents the first day of sobriety and a commitment to recovery.) My food was still out of control and in NA that's okay. It's almost accepted that when you get clean you will overeat and gain weight, so I found no help for my food addiction there. In November I went to my first North Carolina OA meeting. The meetings were small and I was not inspired, so I mainly went to NA. But by the middle of 1996 I was really hurting with my food addiction, so I started driving an hour and a half each way to OA meetings in Charlotte.

It was here that I first heard about the book *Food Addiction: The Body Knows*. A lovely lady in OA gently suggested that I read the book and she loaned me her copy. Here was something that spoke to me. The book described me in a way that none of the OA literature had ever done. I immediately bought my own copy and started on the Recovery Food Plan. I had no real support for this, although I did get an OA sponsor and she acknowledged my plan. She thought it sounded awfully rigid. I stayed on it for five months, lost weight and felt great, but started playing around with portions and food items and eventually relapsed. But the relapses were so bad that I kept going back to the plan. Eventually I heard through the Internet about another Twelve-Step program that used a plan almost identical to the one I was using. I later learned that they used an earlier version of the Plan. I began a lot of e-mail friendships with these food addicts and through them contacted Kay Sheppard.

So I wrote Kay an e-mail and much to my delight she wrote back. I told her a little bit of my food history and then she asked if I wanted to turn my food over to her through e-mail. I hadn't reported my food to anyone in a long time, especially not to the person who had written the plan! I was terrified, but did it anyway. Things would go great for a while; I would get abstinent and lose weight, start sharing in OA about how great my recovery was and then I would start drifting. I would stop weighing and measuring, just eyeballing my portions. My justification was always, "I'm not eating flour, sugar or wheat so it's okay." Then I would start eating out and ordering things that were questionable. Before long I would send my e-mail food plan report and not adhere to it. I had too much pride to stop reporting it, but I was really back in the disease and just lying about it. Eventually, I ended up back in the sugar and wheat. It was always pure hell. I would report my food and then go off on a two-, three- or four-week binge. Eventually, I would be hurting so much that I would e-mail Kay again and ask to start over. She always took me back. Then I would do it all over again. This went on for about two years, the abstinence/relapse cycle. During this time I was in and out of the program, but I stopped going altogether in 1998. Several times during this period I talked about going to a workshop and getting clean, but I never was able to pull it together. I knew it was something that I needed to do, but I was both afraid and resentful that I needed to do it.

My eating was really affecting my life during this time, too. I would have wheat and sugar hangovers that were so severe that I would call in sick to work. I would cancel plans because I'd rather stay home and eat, or because I was feeling so bad from last night's binge. My self-esteem plummeted as I got further and further into the disease. I would pull out of it for a few weeks, but it never lasted.

Eventually, I started putting on a lot of weight after having been at a reasonably healthy weight for many years. I was almost back up to my pre-therapy weight of two hundred eighty-five pounds. I was once again buying Big Men's sizes. My self-image was through the floor. I couldn't even look at myself in the mirror. I was definitely in a state of misery, panic and denial. On the one hand I was very strong in NA–going to lots of meetings, sponsoring, holding service positions–but it was obvious even to my NA friends that something was wrong. So I began sharing at NA about my food addiction. Most didn't get it, but a few did and were supportive. After all, in NA we say in the First Step, "We admitted we were powerless over our addiction;" not drugs, not alcohol, but our addiction. I used NA to survive and it kept me alive. I prayed a lot and asked for relief from my food addiction constantly. But I guess it wasn't going to be as easy as that. I still didn't seem to be willing to do my part.

A good OA friend kindly suggested that maybe I should consider seeking treatment for my eating disorder. I got really angry at her over this. I wasn't "that sick," and was sure I'd be okay if I could get back on the food plan one more time. But in September, I hit a very low bottom with my food. I was emotionally exhausted from all the relapses, and I was fat and miserable. I knew I had to do something different or I would end up one of those nine-hundred pound people you see on the news when they cut out the side of a house to get them out. I called Kay and scheduled a five-day recovery session in Florida.

I arrived in Florida full of a lot of fear and the tiniest bit of hope. I had faith that this lady knew what she was doing and that this was part of my Higher Power's plan for me. The trip to the workshop was an absolute miracle. Being there, I got to work through a lot of my denial about my status as a food addict. I finally understood that if I'm going to deal with my addiction, I will need a lot more discipline than I've been willing to give it. Kay helped me see where I had been cutting corners and had not been willing to go to any length with shopping, eating out, cooking, weighing and measuring and putting my food recovery first. I can't say enough about how positive that experience was. I've put aside my ideas about all those years in OA being effective as far as my ability to deal with the illness day by day. Sure, I learned to work the steps in my life, but now I have to be willing to do what it takes to stay abstinent. I never did that before. I was always resentful over weighing and measuring and always planned to go back to my old ways of eating eventually. I no longer have that reservation. I began to see that this thing is going to kill me if I don't take it seriously. Kay said, "It is really a medical condition that we treat with an abstinent food plan combined with living a Twelve-Step way of life." I realized how many things I'm addicted to: diet sodas, coffee, volume eating, rapid eating, the taste of "sweet" and more. So I made the choice to get rid of those things just for today.

I am enjoying the best clean abstinence I've ever had in my thirteen-plus years of recovery. Every day is an awakening. I'm still coming out of the fog of active addiction, but my feelings and perspectives are slowly falling into place.

This is a totally new way of life, not just a food plan. It involves planning, commitment and focus. It also requires persistence! It's been difficult to find other recovering addicts in my area, so I drive to a meeting once a week that is an hour and a half from my home. Hopefully I'll be able to start a meeting where I live, but it's hard to find people that have truly reached the end of the line with their addiction, who are willing to listen to the truth. It's so important to have good information; now that I see the true nature of the illness so much more clearly, I realize how many years I was operating under misinformation about the biochemical nature of food addiction. It is like being in a land where the food supply has been poisoned and I have to be extremely aware of every bite that crosses my lips. I have been lied to by the endless parade of TV commercials, and the long aisles of addictive foods at the grocery have conspired to lure me into the sickness of addiction. I thank my Higher Power that I found a way out!

I feel good today, peaceful and convinced of the need to work this program every day. I am so grateful to be tasting and enjoying my food again. I'm grateful to have my energy back and to be getting a good night's sleep. I'm grateful to have that wall I built between God and me come tumbling down.

Pierre's Story

He knew he was in trouble with food. Then he lost control and found a recovery program that saved his life.

I had over twenty years of sobriety when food brought me to my knees. I "lost it" at a public function with all of my friends around me. But that wasn't the worst of it. After blowing my stack at the party, I went home and continued the abuse on my wife. The cops were literally knocking on the door ready to take me away when I found recovery from food addiction.

My history was one of blood glucose levels that were out of control. When my blood sugar went high, my temper went out of control, too. For fifteen years the doctors kept warning me that I had to do something about my diabetes. Nothing happened. My family members were very worried. When I came into the program my blood glucose level was three hundred eighty-nine on medication! (Anything over one hundred twenty is considered above normal.) No wonder, I would eat ice cream until my mouth went numb. I would fall asleep sitting in the backyard.

Unbeknownst to me, my wife, who is in recovery, had talked to her sponsor about the abusive situation and had mentioned my diabetic condition. Her sponsor said, "Could he be a food addict?" My wife responded: "A food addict! Of course he is—his room is full of candy bars!" Next thing I knew, I was making a phone call and on my way to a food addiction recovery meeting. I was so relieved and happy to find an answer to my eating and living problems.

They say in AA not to pick up the first drink if your butt falls off. The funny thing is that in recovery from food addiction, my butt did fall off. I wasn't paying much attention to my weight loss when one day my pants fell down. So that is an added benefit (the loss of weight, not the loss of pants!).

But my medical records tell the real story. My blood glucose stays in the normal range and I am off medication. The food plan that my sponsor taught me is the formula for physical recovery, believe me. I keep a record of my daily plan in a spiral book. It strikes me funny that it is called a "Fat Book." Most of the guys in my group carry them. We plan and report our meals to our sponsors.

The first thing my sponsor did for me when we left my first meeting was to take me grocery shopping. I was nervous, but I was really happy when she picked up a container of cut-up mixed melon. I said, "I can have that?" Right then and there, I knew I would be okay on the food plan. My wife supports my recovery and cooked and shopped for me early on. Later I learned to cook for myself and enjoy doing it, too. I had a rough time in grocery stores in the first few months of my program. Now I can shop as well as cook.

My sponsor carries a bunch of bottles in her purse in order to be prepared. Since I don't carry a purse, I figure that I will carry a hip flask for my oil and vinegar dressing. That's a great trade. I used to carry one with booze, now I'll carry one to help me stay abstinent. I take my own salad dressing everywhere with me. I have had some crazy times traveling this past year, but every time I had a delay, I had extra food with me so that I could have an abstinent meal. It was a lucky "mistake" that I had picked up some prepared meals from home the first time I experienced trouble. That airport didn't have anything for me. From then on, I made sure to have extra meals with me. I have needed them every trip, too.

It is wonderful to be starting a new millennium in good

recovery from alcoholism, nicotine addiction, caffeine addiction and food addiction. I work my Steps, lead meetings, pick four or five people up for meetings and make my phone calls. I even report my food plan on the Internet when traveling. I am really glad to be retired because I just can't figure out how people who work can get it all done! Like I say at the end of every meeting: "I'll be back."

2

Food Addiction: A Biogenetic Condition

I Am a Food Addict

Eating until I am stuffed or drugged to sleep;
Not able to predict when the binge will stop;
Craving sticky, pasty, greasy food;
Running out of binge food then frantically searching for another
*   fix;*
Knowing that I am sick and dying;
Scared and angry.
Obsessed with food, obsessed with weight;
Forgetting how bad it was the last time;
Believing food is my friend and comfort;
Eating to feel better–always feeling worse;
Hiding what I eat, where I eat, how much I eat;
Losing control of food and life;
Feeling helpless and hopeless;
Powerless over addictive foods;
Never hungry, never satisfied;
Lying to myself and others;
Having fewer healthy choices;
Sick and tired of being sick and tired;
Questioning why I am so weak;
Dieting, restricting, purging, running, hoping to beat this thing;
Hating how I look and feel;
Wondering if there is a way out;
Binge eating despite the painful consequences;
Wanting less, eating more;
Food is my drug and I am full of shame!

A food addict is a person for whom one bite of binge food is too many and a thousand bites are not enough. Food addiction is a twofold disease: physical intolerance for refined and processed foods, coupled with mental obses-sion. The physical intolerance is a fact–the food addict's body cannot tolerate these foods. One bite will set up a reaction which demands more binge food. Since we act in accordance with our obsessive thoughts, the mental obses-sion commands us to eat, while the physical intolerance condemns us to illness and death. According to Maggie, one of my clients, a food addict is no different from any other kind of addict, except that food is a legal drug which we give to children.

She says, "I am not responsible for having this disease, but I am accountable for treating it. I have an addiction because my body cannot tolerate certain foods. I really don't think people accept my disease in this society. I can't figure out how someone can leave food on their plate, and I am pretty sure that non-food addicts can't understand why I eat so much. Food addicts understand each other. Some of us who are obese wear our pain on the outside. Food addiction is being in hell. I have been discriminated against and ridiculed. When I was in the disease, I was so afraid of life that I stuffed down food until there was nothing left but pain and fat."

For the food addict, binge eating blocks personal growth and maturation as it becomes the addict's only way to cope with life. It is the problem that is perceived as the solution. It is the disease that tells us we don't have a disease. These are the paradoxes of food addiction.

It is a popularly held belief that food addiction is a mental or emotional problem, when actually there is research that indicates it is a physiological or medical condition which adversely affects all areas of life, including emotional and mental stability. As the term food addiction suggests, there is a physiological, biochemical condition of the body which creates craving for refined carbohydrates. The craving and its biochemistry is the same as the alcoholic's craving for alcohol. The need to abstain from the addictive substances is shared by both addictions.

This is something that became clear to Cindy through her own recovery. She says, "I was struggling with food, feelings and myself when I found recovery and the food plan. I also had just started attending a Twelve-Step program. I learned from the food addiction book that it was not my weight but food addiction that was the problem. It was also important for me to understand that the food addict has a metabolic, biochemical imbalance. My brother's imbalance led him to alcohol and drugs. I was determined not to do what he did. You could not pay me to take drugs, but I used my drug—food—for escape and comfort and did not even know it."

Research indicates that food addiction, a biogenetic disease, is inherited just like blue eyes and blond hair. Surprised? Yes, addiction is an inherited trait. Researchers have linked a particular gene to addiction. The findings of addictions specialist Dr. Ernest P. Noble, at the University of California at Los Angeles, focus on a dopamine receptor gene that is responsible for sensations of pleasure or reward. A form of the pleasure gene called A1, previously linked to alcohol and cocaine abuse, may be the cause of carbohydrate craving and compulsive eating. In a study of seventy people who were obese, Dr. Noble and his colleagues found twice as many of them as expected carried the rare dopamine receptor pleasure gene A1. The more common or "normal" gene is the A2.

In previous studies, researchers found the brains of people carrying the rarer A1 gene had fewer dopamine receptors than those with the more common A2 gene. This suggests that people with fewer dopamine receptors may use substances to satisfy the deficit. Just as alcohol and cocaine increase the level of brain dopamine, so do carbohydrates. People eat refined carbohydrates in order to "feel good" by bringing the brain into temporary balance. Food addicts eat highly refined carbohydrates in order to feel better. These carbohydrates increase the level of brain chemicals. Addiction is a process of self-medicating a distressed brain in chemical imbalance.

Food is supposed to make us feel better. We remember the pleasurable after-school "cookies and milk" feeling from childhood. But in addiction, eating to feel better actually makes us feel worse. Why don't the addictive substances keep the addicted brain in balance?

The biochemistry of food addiction follows a path which starts when refined carbohydrates flood the brain with dopamine, serotonin and norepinephrine. As the brain becomes flooded with these neurotransmitters, a feeling of well-being results and craving is stimulated. Serotonin promotes a sense of calm and well-being. It is the brain's own painkiller and tranquilizer. In food addicts, serotonin levels are increased dramatically after the ingestion of refined carbohydrates. In the brain, higher concentrations of serotonin exist in the hypothalamus, which is the site of the basic instincts for food and gratification, and in the limbic system, which deals with emotions. The result is that the food addict walks around "drunk" on refined carbohydrates.

Of course, what goes up must come down. Eventually this carbohydrate flooding creates a neurotransmitter deficiency in the brain. In addiction, it is feast or famine. During the famine, the hypothalamus is affected. Since the hypothalamus is the brain's center for emotions and survival, mood and cravings go out of control. During this process an insufficiency of neurotransmitters leaves receptor sites unfilled. This puts the brain in a condition of imbalance, resulting in distress and depression and cravings. Without additional trigger foods, these lowered feelings can persist for up to twenty-four hours.

It takes increasingly larger and more frequent amounts of carbohydrate to bring the brain back into balance. Over long periods of time, food addicts are unable to get back to baseline. They continue to eat food in order to feel better, but those are exactly the foods which make them feel worse. Those who wish to recover from food addiction need to abstain from those chemicals that trigger the addictive crisis of brain and body chemistry. In recovery, in order to achieve balanced brain chemistry, food addicts learn to be scrupulous about identifying all of the substances that will trigger active addiction.

Who would have thought that it is brain chemistry, not weight, that is the problem? Not those of us who have struggled and attacked our weight in every conceivable way in all those weight-loss programs! Now we see that weight gain is just a symptom of the disease. Have we concentrated too long on weight and weight loss? I think so. The important question instead must be: "Is my eating out of control?" Everywhere we hear weight loss being discussed. Much less often is it suggested that eating addictive foods is the source of weight issues. Those foods and the cravings they trigger have now come under scrutiny. A craving is a powerful urge to get and eat the substances that trigger food addiction. We sometimes hear food addicts calling themselves foodoholics and chocoholics. At this level some understand that what goes on with food addicts is the same as the alcoholic's experience with alcohol.

According to Karen, "Since I have become abstinent from my trigger foods, I have not had any physical cravings for any particular food whatsoever. During this time, there has never been an occasion when I thought that I had to eat something. This is in strong contrast to the cravings that I experienced prior to becoming abstinent. I used to behave exactly like a zombie—I would mechanically purchase and eat whatever my body craved, no matter how fiercely I had promised myself before the craving hit that I would not eat such foods. There was no stopping me from eating whatever came to mind. I had to have it and there was no talking me out of it. The only time I didn't succumb to the cravings immediately was when I was not alone. Then I would find a way to sneak off to eat in isolation. I had absolutely no control over my cravings. They ruled my life like dictators."

Many Terms Describe Food Addiction

What are these eating disorders we hear about so often? There is a category of severely disturbed eating behaviors called eating disorders. These classifications are found in the *Diagnostic and Statistical Manual of Mental Disorders, (DSM-IV)* Fourth Edition. A classification that fits the food addict is *bulimia nervosa*, which is characterized by binge-eating a large amount of high-calorie food, usually carbohydrates, plus inappropriate methods of weight loss or inappropriate methods to avoid weight gain. Bulimics experience loss of control over their eating behaviors. To prevent weight gain from binge eating, bulimics induce vomiting, abuse purgatives such as laxatives and diuretics, restrict food intake between binges, and/or exercise excessively.

There are two subtypes of bulimia nervosa. The first is the purging type, which includes the regular practice of self-induced vomiting and/or the use of purgatives. In some bulimics, vomiting becomes automatic. The second subtype is the nonpurging type, who present a history of food restriction, fasting or immoderate exercise. Bulimia is a description of those who have lost control over the amount they eat. We would call a person of this type a food addict.

Substance Dependence

Food addiction is also viewed as a *substance dependence*. According to the *DSM-IV*, substance dependence is a maladaptive pattern of substance use which leads to clinically significant impairment or distress. It is characterized by tolerance, which is a need for increased amounts of the substance to achieve the desired effect, or a diminished effect with continued use of the same amount of the substance. Secondly, withdrawal is relieved or avoided by use of substances. Next, the substance is often taken in larger amounts over a longer period than was intended. There are persistent and unsuccessful efforts to cut down or control the use of the substance. A great deal of time is spent in activities to obtain the substance, use the substance and recover from its effects. Important social, occupational or recreational activities are given up or reduced because of the use of the substance. Use of the substance is continued despite knowledge of having a persistent or recurrent physical or psychological problem that is likely to have been caused or exacerbated by it. Physiological dependence is evidenced by tolerance or withdrawal syndrome.

Food addicts can surely identify with progression, tolerance and withdrawal. Food addiction is a condition that gets worse over time, involves the use of increasingly more food to get results and produces painful symptoms when the substance is withheld. Much time is spent hiding food, binge eating and getting over the effects of a binge. Bonnie describes this vividly: "In food addiction, I live most days thinking only of where I can get my next fix; of sneaking and hiding food; of wishing everyone would leave the house or get to bed so I can get into my drug of choice and get the 'ahhhhhh' soothing feeling I am after. Talk about insanity! There is no soothing feeling. Instead, I am filled with loathing, self-hate and constant reminders of how I 'sold my soul' once again to this horrible, devastating disease of food addiction."

Night-Eating Syndrome—Another Face of Food Addiction

In August 1999, the *Journal of the American Medical Association* published an article on the behavioral and neuroendocrine characteristics of the night-eating syndrome (NES), which actually appears to be a pattern of food addiction. The person who has night-eating syndrome has little or no appetite for breakfast and delays the first meal of the day for several hours after waking up. This person is not hungry and is often upset about how much was eaten the night before. He or she eats more food after dinner than during the meal, eating more than half of the total daily food after the dinner hour. This person feels tense, anxious, upset or guilty while eating and has trouble falling asleep or staying asleep.

This behavior is not like binge eating, which is done in relatively short episodes. Night-eating syndrome involves continual eating throughout the evening hours. The eating does not provide enjoyment, but produces guilt and shame. In order to meet the diagnostic criteria, this pattern of night eating must have persisted for at least two months.

Amy definitely identified with this aspect of food addiction: "I stayed up to eat at night because my disease had progressed to huge amounts of food intake. At night, no one would see the amounts. They were all asleep. Also, I could not function during the day eating those huge amounts of food. I'd eat until I was on the verge of vomiting, get rid of the containers or wrappers, then pass out in bed. I wouldn't eat until lunchtime because I was usually still full, besides feeling secret horror and shame over how much I ate the night before. I was consuming a gallon of ice cream per night and whatever else I could add to it. It's painful to even think about that behavior. I hadn't thought about the night horror until we started talking about the *JAMA* article. It was unbelievable."

Compulsive Overeating

In some recovery programs food addiction is described by the behavioral component *compulsive overeating*. This implies that both compulsive eating and overeating are indicators of the disorder. If alcoholism were to be described in the same way, the term "compulsive overdrinker" would be used. Although compulsion and overeating are behaviors of the active disease, the underlying biochemistry is addiction –food addiction. Overeating and compulsion are extinguished in good recovery, so many recovering food addicts discontinue the use of such terms to describe themselves. They prefer the term food addict because, "Once a food addict, always a food addict." The biogenetic factor does not change in recovery.

Food Addiction

All of the preceding labels and criteria refer to food addiction, which is loss of control over eating behavior. This term includes the behaviors of binge eating, overeating and compulsive eating. A very high percentage of food addicts have a family history of addiction to various substances. This is not surprising, due to the genetic origin of addiction.

Are You Powerless?

You may be able to identify in your own life the following symptoms of the illness of food addiction.

Do you use food to relieve tension? The addicted person finds temporary relief from aches and pains or emotional tension arising from boredom, anger, depression, self-pity and other emotions.

Are you preoccupied with binge food? Preoccupation often leads addicted people to fortify themselves before a meal or party, sneak more during the meal, avoid non-eating occasions and plan their stash in order to avoid being without binge food.

Do you experience loss of control after the first bite? For an addict, the first bite of an addictive food triggers the compulsion to keep on eating.

Do you blame? Addicts use alibis and rationalizations to excuse unacceptable behavior. This results in blaming abnormal eating behavior on everything and anybody to try and maintain dwindling self-esteem.

Do you get angry if someone questions your eating behavior? Addicts show a growth of irrational behavior patterns, including hostility toward those who show concern, often followed by gestures to make up for such behavior.

Are you lonely? Addiction leads to a breakdown in human relations, which may result in decreasing involvement with family and associates and lead to painful isolation.

Do you have health problems as a result of your eating behavior? Increasing physical disability, including lethargy, interferes with daily activities. Vital organs such as the heart, liver and brain degenerate, requiring hospitalizations, surgery and other medical intervention.

Does your life feel unmanageable? Loss of spiritual contact and feelings of being a "bad person" increase, and a loss of faith results. A sense of failure prevails. These factors contribute to the unmanageability of life. Food addiction adversely affects the addict socially, materially, spiritually and emotionally.

If you are wondering whether you are a food addict, you may wish to answer the following questions. These will help identify a food addiction problem:

- Has anyone ever told you that you have a problem with food?
- Do you think food is a problem for you?
- Do you eat large amounts of high-calorie food in short amounts of time?
- Do you eat to numb your feelings?
- Can you stop eating whenever you wish?
- Has your eating or weight ever interfered with your jobs, relationships or finances?
- How often do you weigh yourself?
- Do you judge yourself by the number on your scale?

- Do you often eat more than you planned to eat?
- Have you hidden food or eaten in secret?
- Have you become angry when someone eats food you have put aside for yourself?
- Have you ever been anxious about your size, shape or weight?
- How many weight-loss programs have you tried?
- List all of the ways you have attempted to lose weight.
- Do you manipulate ways to be alone so that you can eat privately?
- Do your friends and companions overeat or binge eat?
- How often do you overeat?
- Are other members of your family, including parents, siblings, aunts, uncles and grandparents, addicted to food, alcohol, nicotine or drugs?
- Do you often feel guilty about the amount you eat?
- Do you frequently think about food?
- Have you ever thought you should cut down on your eating?
- Has anyone ever annoyed you by criticizing your eating?
- Have you ever felt guilty about your eating?
- Have you ever eaten for emotional relief?

If your answers to these questions concern you, seek guidance. Remember, recovery begins with self-knowledge. Identification of the problem–realizing that something is wrong–leads to recovery. Help is available. Hope, in the form of a recovery plan, is what this book can offer you.

3

Self-Medicating with Addictive Substances

Addictive substances are forms of plant life which have been refined or processed in order to be ingested by drinking, eating, inhaling or injecting. The refinement process facilitates quick absorption of substances which effectively alter brain chemistry and change mood by flooding the brain with neurotransmitters, which are brain chemicals such as serotonin and dopamine. Food addicts seek this mood change by eating refined and processed carbohydrate and fatty foods which result in a short-term "high." But what goes up must come down, and the high is followed by a long period of depressed feelings. In order to avoid these lowered feelings, the addict eats more. "More is better" is the addict's slogan.

The refined and processed foods that serve as drugs of choice for food addicts are usually mixtures of sugar, flour, caffeine and fats—including baked goods, sweets, fast foods, everything chocolate, sweetened drinks and snack foods.

Food addicts self-medicate with these addictive foods because they provide temporary relief from distressed brain chemistry. Food substances that change brain chemistry and alter mood are sugar, flour, wheat, fat, caffeine and alcohol, plus volume and personal binge foods. Any substance that alters mood has addictive potential. Our experience proves that the following substances are addictive for people who are genetically predisposed to food addiction.

Sugar Blues

We abstain from all forms of sugar, which floods the brain with serotonin and raises endorphin levels. Sugar hides

under many different names. It is very important to understand that food processors are creative in their many ways
of concealing sugar in the products we eat—even the ones
that are called sugar-free.

Why is sugar such a secret? Processors know that sugar
makes folks buy more. Labels that say sugar-free really
mean sugar-full! Avoid all products that have such a caption
on the label. Processors can say a product is sugar-free if it
does not contain sucrose. However, it may contain other
forms of sugar such as maltodextrose or polydextrose.
Refined carbohydrates have many pseudonyms, and we
must begin to recognize the attempts to mislead. Sugar by
any other name will still trigger the addictive process.

For instance, in the past year or two, the ingredient
"whey" has shown up with increasing frequency. Most of us
know vaguely that whey is a dairy product and that Little
Miss Muffet ate it, but what exactly is it? "You know, whey
is the liquid part of cottage cheese," people would say when
I asked. Upon investigation, we found that whey is a sugar.
It doesn't look like sugar on the label, so many people are
deceived. But a researcher eventually supplied the answer—
whey is seventy-one percent lactose. There it is! Whey is
nearly three-fourths sugar.

Now there is an even newer kid on the block which is
showing up on labels—"natural flavors." Avoid products with
this ingredient unless you call the processor to identify
which "natural flavor" is being used. Experience has shown
that this may be some kind of sugar lurking under an innocent name. Be alert for sugars with words that end in "ose,"
"ol" and "syrup." (See Appendix I for a complete list of the

names of sugar.) Since it would be impossible to identify all of them, the rule of thumb is that when you do not recognize an ingredient, leave that product in the store. I recently examined a "sugar-free" cough preparation and found its first listed ingredient to be Ace K. Surprise! The first name on our sugar list is Ace K. It's a full-time job keeping track of the names of sugar.

Flour, Sugar's Next-Door Neighbor

Flour is a highly refined carbohydrate closely related to sugar. It is a high-carbohydrate grain product which acts in an addictive manner due to the refinement process. Refinement increases the speed with which the substance moves through the bloodstream and into the brain where it does its work. When flour is eaten, it is absorbed into the bloodstream through the walls of the stomach and small intestine. Refinement increases the absorption rate of this food, which changes brain chemistry and alters mood. Not wanting to risk inhaling flour particles while sifting and pouring, consider giving up the practice of cooking and baking with this drug.

When we talk of flour, we mean every kind of flour there is: rice flour, oat flour, brown flour, white flour, cornmeal. The complex natural grains are great. These are slowly absorbed. But if it is a ground-up, powdered grain—abstain! These highly refined carbohydrates flood the brain with serotonin, which acts like a tranquilizer and a painkiller. No wonder we are numb after bingeing on this product.

Wheat, the Opiate

Marty's recovery was a struggle until she found out about wheat abstinence. She writes: "I could never maintain any kind of appropriate abstinence just abstaining from sugar. Worse yet was that impossible attempt to eat three balanced meals a day with nothing in between. I had to get rid of those wheat products. They kept me crazy. The awful thing was that I only ate about three things that contained wheat, anyway. Why didn't I realize they set me off? I am glad I found out eventually. Life is good on wheat abstinence. I am glad to know it today!"

Research indicates that when food proteins such as wheat gluten are digested, small peptides with opioid properties are produced and absorbed. They are called exorphins to distinguish them from the endorphins usually found in the body. Endorphins are produced in the body and exorphins come from external sources such as food. Remember, morphine and heroin are also opioids.

Research into food allergies has shown that many people develop intolerances to particular foods. Wheat leads the list of these foods. The term intolerance rather than allergy is used, because in many cases the immune system may not be involved. We learned in AA literature that we have a physical allergy coupled with a mental obsession. With a slight revision based on current research, we might say we have a physical intolerance coupled with a mental obsession. Referring to wheat, J. Egger (1988) says, "One of the most striking phenomenon in these studies is that patients often exhibit cravings, addiction and withdrawal symptoms with regard to these foods." See Appendix II for a complete list of the names of wheat and flour products.

Fats Are Mood-Altering, Too

Fat is a mind-blowing, mood-altering, crazy-making substance. I never would have known this except that, when I started abstaining from everything else, it called out so loudly to be eaten and in some circumstances to be drunk. Clean abstinence tells its own story about substances. Without it, I would never have been able to identify my personal problem foods.

From my own experience and the experiences of others in good clean abstinence, I can clearly see that animal fats are highly risky. A former patient told me about her experience with an animal fat product that took over her life. She was in a well-known fast food restaurant and decided to have a decaf coffee. She chose to use half and half instead of low-fat milk. After that occasion, she found herself in that fast food joint frequently adding half and half to her decaf. She finally realized that it had to go when she found herself drinking the stuff straight by the glassful.

Nuts and seeds are tricky high-fat foods as well. I remember a client in group therapy shouting out, "Nuts drive me nuts!" Nuts and seeds are little blobs of fat with a small amount of carbohydrate and protein. Plaster them with salt and the binge food is complete. Roast them in more fat and you have a real suicide food.

So what is it about fat that is so addictive? It is those

endorphins which are brain chemicals that act like painkillers. Just like other addictive substances, fats release endorphins which change brain chemistry and alter mood. When we lose control over this substance we can trace it back to those morphine-like substances in the brain.

Caffeine Highs

Caffeine is a xanthine derivative substance which results in withdrawal symptoms of headache, severe fatigue, stomach upsets and irritability. The addictive use of caffeine induces central nervous system intoxication, habituation, tolerance and withdrawal when use is discontinued. Using caffeine results in hyperactivity, irritability, insomnia, dehydration and possibly heartburn. I have witnessed extreme cases of withdrawal. In one, a client slept almost continuously for five days. A friend, who was a heavy caffeine user of several pots of coffee per day, reported experiencing hallucinations during her withdrawal period.

The chemicals in coffee include many which are toxic and allergenic. Coffee is not the only source of caffeine; tea, soft drinks, chocolate and over-the-counter medications also contribute to the intake of this substance. The use of this substance is usually minimized. The pleasures of caffeine abstinence include genuine rest and authentic energy rather than the false sense of energy produced by caffeine.

Chocolate, which contains caffeine, is usually combined with all of the addictive food substances in the form of candy and baked goods. It is a powerful substance which has both stimulant and antidepressant effects.

Alcohol

You may be surprised to see that alcohol is listed as a trigger food. Libraries of books have been written about the addictive potential of alcohol. We might not identify ourselves as alcoholics or alcohol abusers, though some of us may be, but alcohol is a highly refined carbohydrate that will flip on the switch of food addiction. Alcohol effectively triggers food addiction like any other refined carbohydrate. It is, in fact, the most highly refined carbohydrate. Like sugar, alcohol floods the brain with serotonin. Think of it as liquid sugar. Remember the line by Ogden Nash: "Candy is dandy but liquor is quicker." When it comes to mood alteration and effect on judgment, truer words were never spoken.

Alcohol is an addictive substance to guard against and eliminate for good clean abstinence. Even if we are not drinkers, it is safest to be on guard against alcoholic extracts, restaurant foods prepared with wines and liquors, and alcohol in toothpaste and mouthwash. Remember that substances can be absorbed through the mucous membrane of the mouth. That is how some medications are administered, such as nitroglycerin which is placed under the tongue. It is best to be cautious and keep our mouths alcohol-free.

Volume

Bingeing on a large amount of food is common for food addicts. We must include volume on our list of things from which we abstain. Even in recovery, your body will recognize a high intake of carbohydrates and fat and the disease will be triggered accordingly. Cups and scales used to weigh and measure are our tools to manage volume. Yes, we even tote our measuring devices to restaurants. Why open the door to the disease in a building full of addictive food choices? Malcolm says, "Yesterday was a good day. I ate out with my buddies and showed them my scale and explained my plan. It went well. I was very nervous going in, but I just told them up front the whole story. They wanted to know what kind of plan I was on. I explained that it's a food plan written by a recovering addict. They were pretty impressed and very understanding. Anyway, it's getting easier to eat out, the more I practice it." Increasing volume is one of the first signs of relapse.

Personal Binge Foods

Identifying personal binge foods is a challenge to be worked through with a sponsor. When a person is strictly adhering to the food plan and cravings persist, (physical urges, not mental obsessions) the triggering foods must be identified and eliminated. They may be allergenic or addictive foods. Keeping a daily record of foods eaten will aid in the identification of these personal triggers. For instance, "I have cravings every Monday when I eat corn. Corn must be the culprit!" This kind of food review leads to the elimination of personal binge foods.

The other category of personal binge foods is those foods which are high in simple sugars, such as fruit, and processed carbohydrates, such as oatmeal. Such foods may act in an addictive way for individuals who are highly carbohydrate sensitive. For others, starchy vegetables such as carrots and potatoes may be problematic. It is important to vary the selection of foods on a rotating basis. Any food that is used on a daily basis is suspect despite the tempting rationalization that it is quick or convenient.

"Quick" and "instant" foods are always too highly processed. These forms of grains and starches may well trigger an addictive response. Select the least refined form of grains and starches–these are slowly digested and absorbed.

Finally, there is a certain emotional issue related to personal binge foods. If a certain food is "allowed" on the food plan, it seems that we ought to be able to handle it. This is just not so. Constant vigilance and awareness, plus an honest desire to stay abstinent, are necessary to maintain recovery. We may have to eliminate personal binge foods from time to time. Clean abstinence and peace of mind is worth the effort and sacrifice.

Consequences of Self-Medicating with Addictive Substances

Men and women with physical intolerance to mind-altering foods and chemicals, who compulsively persist in their use, have a disease. This disease is addiction. It has recognizable symptoms and a predictable progression. Continued use of the addictive substances produces loss of control–"powerlessness." The physical need for the food of choice grows, as does the inability to operate without it. As we have seen, this medical condition, addiction, leads to self-medication with the addictive substances.

When food addicts use food to relieve tension, they find only temporary relief from pain, followed by increased pain and anguish. The consequences of treating our disease with addictive substances are overwhelmingly negative. This self-medicating form of treatment has been exposed as a failure by every recovering person when the direct consequences of the use of addictive substances are evaluated. Every person has his or her own list of outcomes. Identifying these consequences is the way it is proven to the addict that life in addiction is "unmanageable." We eventually see that food addiction negatively affects every area of life: family, social, occupational, financial and spiritual; plus mental, emotional and physical health.

Mental difficulties and physical misery are caused by alternating bingeing and dieting or purging. The use of addictive foods aggravates and creates medical conditions such as obesity, arthritis, diabetes, migraine headaches and certain heart conditions, to name a few. See Appendix III for a list, developed by Dr. Nancy Appleton, of the medical complications. Physiological conditions involving the heart, respiration, kidneys, gallbladder and circulatory system are negatively affected by the addictive process. Increasing physical disability, including lethargy, interferes with daily activities; vital organs such as the heart, liver and brain degenerate, requiring hospitalizations, surgery and other medical intervention.

Our hospitals are full of people whose eating is out of control. Obesity is an epidemic that has increased dramatically in the past ten years. It now affects nearly one in five adults and kills an estimated three hundred thousand or more a year, according to recent studies in the *Journal of the American Medical Association*. Obesity receives the most attention, but underweight and normal-sized food addicts are sick and dying from food addiction, too.

It is not unusual for food addicts to be alternately depressed, anxious or full of rage. The result can be diagnoses and medications that have little effect on the primary diagnosis and no effect on the addictive process at all. Not to be confused with true dual-diagnosis patients, food addicts present with medications for multiple diagnoses which frequently clear up in abstinent recovery.

Social, occupational and family life is disrupted by addiction. The food addict experiences financial difficulties due to unemployment or underemployment, the cost of binge food, weight-loss programs, medical treatment and therapy.

Isolation, unresolved conflicts and resentments lead to the decline in all these areas of life. The addicted person sneaks, steals and protects his or her stash. Food addicts live with shame, humiliation, guilt and loss of self-esteem. Tina says, "I was plagued by the shame that accompanies closet binge eating and the insecurity that results from carrying a large amount of excess weight." The use of alibis and rationalizations to excuse unacceptable behavior results in blaming abnormal eating behavior on everything and anybody in an attempt to maintain decreasing self-esteem. There is a growth of irrational behavior patterns, including anger and hostility toward those who show concern. Breakdown in human relations often results in decreasing involvement with family and associates, leading to painful isolation. Reaching for substances instead of for help creates a sense of separation from God and humankind. Loss of spiritual contact and feelings of being a "bad person" increase, and the loss of faith results. A sense of failure prevails. All of these factors contribute to the unmanageability of a food addict's life. Recognition of the pain leads to recovery.

4

The Beginning of Recovery

Changing Our Thinking

In recovery, we change the way we think about food. It is not a comfort, a friend or a solution. We may have called certain foods "comfort food." That was deluded, because those foods never created comfort for us. In fact, they created our private hells. When we think of the consequences of turning to food for comfort and relief, we need to recall the physical, mental, emotional and spiritual consequences of using food addictively. We used to call food from the bakery "goodies." Those items were not good to us at all. They caused irritability, lethargy, medical problems, depression, obesity and a whole host of maladies. It was habitual to turn to food instead of God, loved ones or counselors. That is the major transgression of the disease. People in good recovery must guard against subtle ways of turning to food for solace.

The Grief Process

Winnie shared at a meeting that she had sobbed through her first abstinent holiday season, hiding in closets, crying with friends and relatives. She was in the grief process. With less than a year in recovery, she was in the withdrawal and post-acute withdrawal period. Grief is part of that cycle. It is an emotional reaction to a major loss—the loss of a way of life.

Elisabeth Kübler-Ross identified the stages of the grief process: denial, anger, bargaining, depression, acceptance. When Winnie came into recovery, she let go of her whole way of life. It had been a predictable path filled with deluded ideas and unhealthy attachments, but she did not see it that way. She thought food was her friend and lover. Then she entered the first stage of grief, which is denial. The old delusions surfaced and she fondly recalled the days of her addiction. She was the best cook, baker and eater in the crowd. Then she began to see that in order to achieve abstinence she would have to release people, places and pastimes. She had depended on the substances that caused her suffering. "How vulnerable I am without my drug!" she cried. "I am losing my drug and my identity."

Winnie took one step forward when she began to see that the drug created her suffering. She ate to feel better and it made her feel worse. She talked about it with her sponsor and at meetings. She listened to others share. Then she moved into the next stage of grief, which is anger. "Why am I a food addict? Why me? Why can't I eat like everyone else?" she screamed. She took out her anger on her family with verbal arguments. She blamed her husband and other relatives for her unhappiness. Her home became a battleground. She continued to work with her sponsor, eventually taking responsibility for her feelings by working the steps and evaluating her tendency to judge, criticize and blame.

Winnie then entered the next phase of grief, which is the bargaining stage. When faced with the evidence that certain foods had caused enormous injury, she started to negotiate with the food plan and browse for substitutes. "I will give up sugar, flour and wheat, but surely I can continue to have my favorites when I go to the movies." She wandered about the health food store looking for "abstinent" bread, crackers and cookies.

Continuing to work with a sponsor and attend meetings, she chose to become accountable and committed to a clean food plan. She let go of control and accepted the solution. At this point she entered the stage of sadness. She could see that she had lost a lot while in the disease process. She began facing reality and living life on life's terms without food to medicate. She realized that the gift of recovery sat upon the foundation of sacrifice of the old ways. Deeply saddened by the knowledge that her participation in family traditions and functions would never be the same again, she understood that she was no longer going to be part of the food fest. From now on she would be the different one, no longer being one of the gang. She felt sad and afraid, but continued to talk about her feelings with her sponsor and at meetings, identifying with others who felt the same.

Eventually her sadness gave way to acceptance. With acceptance, her grief process ended. Eventually, Winnie could say with firm resolution, "I never gave up a thing. I was relieved of a lot of painful consequences when I let go of food. In recovery I am being deprived of obesity, insanity, shame, secret eating, dishonesty, heartburn and a few other unattractive features of this disease."

One Day at a Time

The idea that each day is a new beginning "cleans the slate" every twenty-four hours. What a great idea–to start fresh each day, rather than getting bogged down in old ideas, condemning ourselves for past mistakes and failures, or worse yet, repeating them! The AA book reads, "We held onto our old ideas and the result was nil until we let go absolutely." We can let go of our self-defeating ideas and replace them with self-enhancing ones. That is a positive new beginning. Set up a daily recovery goal for yourself and attain it, no matter what.

This idea of new beginnings is based on the hope that we can grow and change, and the idea that growth takes place in the everlasting "here and now." One of the first things I heard in recovery rooms was, "The past is a canceled check, the future is a promissory note, the present is ready cash. Spend it well!" Power is in the moment, and what we do with it will create the pattern of our lives.

Another old recovery saying is, "You can't recover on yesterday's program." We can decide to do our recovery "thing" today–or not do it. It is important to know just exactly what the recovery program is going to be today. Some options on a daily basis are:

- contact sponsor
- attend a meeting
- exercise
- journal
- meditate
- pray

- adhere to food plan
- make phone calls
- read recovery literature
- practice the Twelve Steps

We need to determine our best recovery program in order to actually do it. Next, make selections for a "To Do Today" list. Which recovery behaviors are most needed right now? Whatever those choices might be, the assignment is to "Just do it." A good question to ask each day is, "What Step am I working on today?" The answer is really based on the outcome of inventory work. A crucial recovery tool is the daily inventory. The only way to avoid relapse is to take frequent inventories to identify barriers to recovery and warning signs of relapse. The relapse process is part of the recovery process which will, if unchecked, take us back into the disease of addiction. Little daily lapses lead to painful full-blown relapses. Stop them in their tracks with daily inventory to evaluate and correct relapse traps. Remember—relapse happens in the absence of an active recovery program.

Power is in the here and now. That is where we meet our Higher Power, in the present. The only way for us to practice the presence of God is to be fully conscious in the moment. "There is One who has all power—that one is God. May you find him now!" reads the *Alcoholics Anonymous* book. I need to keep finding the God of my understanding, to invite the Power into my life and to raise my consciousness of God's gifts of peace and serenity. All my new beginnings have been because of God's grace.

Just for today I will let go of old ideas.
Just for today I will work my program.
Just for today I will take a personal inventory.
Just for today I will correct past errors.
Just for today I will invite God into my life.

Choices

Recovery is a choice; no one can do it for us. The foundation of recovery from food addiction is making appropriate food choices on a daily basis. Since we have to eat every day, we have an ongoing need to check the contents of the food that we eat, with the goal of using only food that is free of sugar, flour, wheat and other identified trigger foods. This constitutes our personal commitment to recovery and can be achieved by planning, reading labels and asking questions.

The result of good choices is a body free of all substances which will trigger an addictive response. Recovery is a continual effort. To ensure ongoing abstinence, it is essential to identify all substances which will trigger the disease process. Food addiction is a progressive disease, therefore the identification of appropriate and effective food choices is highly subjective and perpetual–it is a lifetime endeavor. As the disease progresses, it is likely that we become more carbohydrate sensitive, not less. It is for this reason that food choices must be reviewed for current appropriateness. All food plans are guidelines to physical recovery. Not only do our bodies change, but manufacturers change recipes and ingredients. Checking for these factors by examining labels is quality control for the food addict.

Overcoming Denial

Denial is a major symptom of addictions, including food addiction. It is a psychological mechanism humans use to protect themselves from fear by blocking the awareness of truth. Denial by food addicts consists of blocking the awareness of excessive and inappropriate use of food and the resulting harmful consequences. Denial is a potentially fatal aspect of food addiction because it impairs judgment and results in self-delusion, locking the addict into a destructive pattern.

Dee's denial took the form of listing symptoms she didn't have while overlooking those that pointed to food addiction. She tells us, "My biggest stumbling block was denial about my disease. I couldn't identify myself as someone with an eating disorder. My denial continued as I read anecdotes about food addicts. The examples usually talked about someone who was a fat kid, which I wasn't; or purged, which I didn't; or ate amazing quantities of food, which I didn't; or went on starvation diets, and I didn't do that either. How could I be a food addict? I wasn't like those people. I gained weight slowly and steadily until, after two pregnancies, I was about forty pounds overweight. I thought I was eating well. My diet consisted of pasta with veggies, shredded wheat and bananas. I never 'crash-dieted.' I snacked on fruit, popcorn and pretzels. I thought I was eating like a normal, healthy person. I didn't realize that I was an addict because my foods of choice seemed to be healthy. Now I know otherwise. Those food choices would trigger binges. I didn't understand why I was hungry so soon after I ate. At the time I thought it was hunger, but now I know it was craving. And if I had a craving for a sweet, I would have just a few cookies, not a whole box. But little by little they added up. Until I got abstinent I couldn't see what I was doing. A handful of raisins, a cup of sugar-free yogurt and a bunch of grapes are sugar binges, just the same as a box of cookies!"

Denial permits the addict to ignore medical advice such as, "Stop overeating or you will die!" Recently I heard a heart patient who had just undergone quadruple-bypass surgery say with a laugh, "Why live if I can't eat what I want?" Addiction, through the mechanism of denial, creates a value system in which the use of the substances overrides the will to live. This heart patient was in that trap and didn't even know it.

A woman weighing over four hundred pounds who is in denial says, "I can lose weight any time I want to. I just don't want to." Denial is the term used for a wide variety of psychological defenses which food addicts unwittingly set up to protect themselves from realizing they are addicted. All of these defenses distort reality. For instance, in simple denial the addict maintains that something true is not true. This dishonesty is a form of denial, although the addict is not aware of it. "Who ate the bag of cookies?" "I don't know!" Of course, I know I ate them, but eventually I actually begin to believe my own lies. One food addict says, "I would steal my children's candy and then sit back and watch as they fought and accused each other."

At other times we minimize the situation by admitting the problem in such a way that it appears to be insignificant. "All I need is a good diet plan and everything will be all right." Another method of denial is to give up responsibility entirely by blaming and projecting responsibility onto someone or something else. The behavior is not denied, but its cause is identified as an external person, place or thing. "You would overeat, too, if you had a husband (children, mother, job) like mine!"

Everyone knows about rationalizing, that is, making alibis and excuses for behavior. Rationalizing and justifying are attempts to create a logical reason for illogical behavior. "I was in so much pain, naturally I ate for comfort." Since food addicts eat to feel better and then feel worse, this idea is irrational. While active in the disease, we just don't see it that way. All of these defenses protect and preserve the disease process and defend against healthy recovery.

When an addict moves into compliance, he or she agrees to follow a suggested path with the hope that life will improve. This demonstrates a show of trust in sponsors, therapists and recovering people in support groups. This trust leads to surrender, and surrender leads to acceptance.

Recovery begins with confrontation and breakdown of the addict's denial system. Often addicts think they are being attacked when their denial is confronted, but actually the disease, not the person, is confronted. Support people join the addict in this confrontation. It is important to know that the disease is being challenged, not the person. Confrontation does not mean attack; it is the objective description of what is seen and heard. For instance, "You don't think you are a food addict despite the fact that you are a hundred and fifty pounds overweight."

It is a challenge to separate "disease thinking" from "recovery thinking." Learning to recognize and confront "old ideas" that will lead back into the disease is a major challenge of recovery.

Stages of Recovery

It is important to learn to understand the early stages of recovery. Developmentally, recovery occurs in stages—early, middle and late. Each stage of recovery involves certain tasks to be completed. The most serious block to moving through the developmental stages is picking up the primary addictive substance. This stops all progress. In food addiction recovery, we see this happen frequently. It is sad to see people struggle to get a few days, weeks or months of abstinence, only to return to trigger foods and binge eating over and over again—never completing withdrawal and never getting stabilized.

The person who establishes this pattern continues to suffer from the disease and from withdrawal symptoms on an ongoing basis. I call this the Zero-One Syndrome. Step Zero is being in active disease. Step One is the first phase of recovery, which includes establishing abstinence and experiencing withdrawal. Going back and forth in a pattern of disease and withdrawal is not pleasant. Completing withdrawal and becoming stabilized is dependent on maintaining complete abstinence from addictive substances.

Another confounding issue concerning the completion of the stages of recovery from addiction is that people are often poly-addicted. As they are moving through the developmental stages and completing the associated tasks, other addictions are progressing, increasing and getting worse. These other addictions are a serious block to progress in recovery from primary addiction. Food addicts who visit AA meetings often comment about the sweets, caffeine and nicotine used by the members. The possibility that some AA members are addicted to one or more of these substances is likely. Remembering the genetic basis of addiction, it is a distinct probability that the use of such substances by alcoholics is addictive. For food addicts, the coexisting addictions can be shopping/spending; other addictive substances such as alcohol, caffeine, nicotine and prescription drugs; as well as relationship and sex addictions.

The first stage of recovery is convalescence. Treat early recovery as a recuperation period. This is a time to practice the slogan "Easy Does It." It is not the time to take on new endeavors, part-time jobs, extra college courses or other stressors that might seem like a good idea at the time. We get into recovery and feel so great it is tempting to take on extra projects. We want to play catch-up to remedy all those things we missed during active disease. The reality is that it takes from a year to eighteen months to stabilize physically. We have brought all of the consequences of our disease right along with us. Our bodies start operating in a different mode, needing to overcome years of tension, fatigue, isolation and poor nutrition which have created a low tolerance for further stress. Be a realist by resisting temptations and demands to perform beyond your current abilities. Good nutrition which includes supplementing vitamins and minerals, adequate rest and relaxation, and involvement in a Twelve-Step fellowship are remedies for years of neglect. Another slogan fits the bill here: "First Things First," remembering recovery is always first. The goal of recovery is bringing the body, mind and spirit into balance. Healthy choices restore brain chemistry balance.

Tasks of Early Recovery

Completing Withdrawal. This is accomplished by staying on a food plan that works and eliminating all addictive food substances, including personal trigger foods and volume. Managing acute and post-acute withdrawal symptoms is a challenge in the early days. Short-term symptoms may be flu-like, including chills, muscle aches, irritability, anxiety, insomnia, frequent urination and nausea. The acute phase usually lasts from three to ten days. Beyond that, post-acute withdrawal symptoms may occur during the first year. Usually we are not prepared for post-acute withdrawal. Often regarded as "having a really bad time," these later withdrawal symptoms are likely to occur around monthly anniversary dates in the third, sixth or ninth month and during times of stress. Healthful choices which help to establish physical, emotional and spiritual balance are the tools that counter post-acute withdrawal symptoms.

Learning to Be Abstinent. In the first days of recovery it is important to work with a sponsor to learn how to be abstinent by recognizing and eliminating the addictive substances, reading labels and locating appropriate food sources. You may wish to ask your sponsor to shop with you in the grocery store and the health food store in order to make suitable food selections.

Food Plan Management. This is a very important task of early recovery. Planning, reporting and committing food to a sponsor is an effective way to learn to manage food. Make a commitment to weigh and measure in order to control volume; schedule meals on a regular basis to maintain a level metabolism. We develop our plan for life during the early days.

Developing a Support Network. Our helping networks will include other recovering people, therapists, spiritual advisors, family members and other supportive people. It is a basic task of recovery to choose helpful, understanding people to be part of this network, which we will continue to build in future years.

Orientation and Participation in Twelve-Step Programs. We establish a pattern of attending meetings and learn about the Twelve-Step way of life. Regular attendance at meetings and establishing a home group will end isolation. We become part of a fellowship that offers shared experience, strength and hope.

Combating Obsession with Food. In recovery we get the idea that we are powerless to control many things, including people, places, situations and things outside ourselves. We can control what we see, what we think, what we say and what we do. In that regard, we develop tools for managing obsessive thoughts of food. Obsession is mental. We can control our thoughts. How do we suppress the old habitual thoughts of binge food that come to mind or thoughts that rationalize the next spontaneous bite? We think it through.

Patty was planning to go to a retreat in a few weeks. She thought, *I may as well binge until the retreat and then get abstinent there.* She wondered, *Where did that thought come from? I have been abstinent for months, why would I sacrifice that for another binge?* Talking with sponsors or therapists helps us understand that nothing positive is accomplished on a binge. Because Patty had done that work, she replaced an old thought with a new one.

Understanding Physical Cravings. Cravings are physical. When experiencing a craving for food, it is critical to examine food eaten in the past twenty-four hours for addictive substances that triggered the craving. Usually food eaten in restaurants or an unchecked ingredient list is the culprit. We cannot be casual about the food we consume. Cravings are too high a price to pay! Check labels, order carefully in restaurants and eat simply at friends' homes. It is better to err on the side of caution than to take chances with abstinence.

Developing Motivation and Commitment. How do we develop motivation and commitment to recovery? As we stabilize in recovery, things get better. We are living instead of just existing. We feel healthier, we become more focused and emotionally settled. We count our blessings. Recovery looks better than the disease process. Motivation follows positive actions. Commitment keeps us going back for more. Those who came before us proclaim the joy of recovery.

From them we learn that recovery is the better way.

Emotional Stabilization Follows Physical Stabilization. Years of shame, guilt, remorse and resentments have taken their toll. During active addiction, we are unable to deal with emotions because we have used our substance to subdue feelings rather than learning ways to deal with them. In this phase of stabilization, it is wise to learn how to identify and express feelings in an appropriate way. Learning and practicing life skills such as problem-solving, coping skills and assertive communication techniques—along with Twelve-Step work—is important to achieving emotional stability. These are appropriate therapeutic and recovery goals for early growth and development.

A word here concerning intense therapy. Many food addicts are never able to stabilize emotionally because their therapy focuses on family of origin, abuse, incest and other such emotionally hot issues. Therapy of this type creates a strong emotional climate that often sends addicts back to their substance for relief. After all, we ate to avoid intense feelings. It is not helpful to open painful core issues early in the process. Stabilization occurs when we focus on changing attitudes and behavior, living in the here and now, and identifying and managing symptoms.

5

A Food Plan
That Works

The First Bite Concept

A recovering alcoholic, an enlightened person, once said, "If you don't pick up the first drink you will never get drunk." What a concept. It makes so much sense. I've also heard it said that, "All you ever give up is just one drink–the first one." That really shrinks the task down to size. There is no way of bypassing the first drink in order to take the second one. That "first drink" philosophy is airtight.

When I came into recovery from food addiction, I heard a similar idea–the "first bite" concept. The slogan was loud and clear: "We don't pick up the first bite." The same logic holds true for food as it does for alcohol. If you don't pick up the first bite, you won't trigger the food addiction process. Pick up the first bite and you are walking around drunk on binge food again. Now that I have had a number of years to think about it, I can see there are a variety of "first bites" from which we abstain–the first compulsive bite, the first spontaneous bite, the first addictive bite. What does this all mean?

The *compulsive bite* occurs when we eat to soothe feelings; that is compulsive eating. The irony here is that we eat to feel better and what we eat makes us feel worse. Eating because of uncomfortable feelings never worked. It may have numbed us for a while, but it never resolved the feelings. Those hurting emotions could be ignored for a while as we ate out of control, but they never went away. The fact that the pain remains causes an increase in the amount and frequency of food necessary to dull the pain. This is an example of progression–food addiction is a progressive disease.

Overeating and volume eating mean disregarding volume control by discarding our scale, cup and measuring spoon. In recovery we no longer eat two or three bowls of food. We use our measuring tools to manage volume. We know too much food will trigger active addiction. We just don't know how many bowls of cereal will do it. If we eat food according to our food plan, we are safe. If we stray, there is no telling what will happen. There is real security in maintaining the structure of the food plan. Those who have relapsed and who then get back into recovery know this fact as a primary element of their future continuing recovery.

The *spontaneous bite* has to do with "permission-giving"– reaching out and eating what we want when we want it. We give ourselves permission to eat a bite of vegetable while we are preparing meals, or we allow an apple in the middle of the afternoon. Since abstinence is based on having a plan and sticking to it, spontaneous eating is obviously not part of our strategy for recovery. Spontaneous eating constitutes a breakdown of discipline and is part of the relapse process. An extra this or that today leads to total loss of control in the future. We have to deal with the insidious "BLTs" (bites, licks and tastes). One person in recovery confides, "I am a bad one for putting things in my mouth while preparing meals, and also I lick utensils." This is a practice that must be abolished. In recovery, we raise awareness of abstinence between meals. Meals are eaten on schedule and at the table in order to place boundaries on our eating. Like it or not, recovery is about discipline. Disciplined eating is a safe way of life in recovery. Planning what to eat, and eating what we plan, is our goal.

The *addictive bite* ends recovery. Above all, we abstain from addictive eating, which is the act of consuming addictive substances. This behavior puts us back into full-blown disease. We know again the meaning of powerlessness; our lives become unmanageable. This is the end of our happiness, joy and freedom. It is an important recovery task to stay free of the substances which will trigger the end of recovery for us. It takes vigilance and awareness to accomplish the kind of clean abstinence we need in order to avoid triggers. Avoidance of triggers constitutes clean abstinence.

Giving Up the Diet Way of Life

You just have to pass through the bookstore or the magazine section of the grocery store to see that our society is obsessed with food and weight. The latest diets are all represented there, new ones every month. The magazine covers have a picture of a really fancy dessert; then down in the corner is a description of the major weight loss that can be accomplished in nothing flat, with no effort at all—and while you are at it, bake a cake, too. Recently the banner on the cover of a popular magazine claimed that you can "Lose thirty-five pounds in thirty minutes." By now we know that diets don't work. Because we are addicts, we have to have something that works for us. When dieting stops, recovery begins.

Complete loss of control over the amount we eat–that is addiction! Losing control doesn't mean that we can't stop eating. It means that we can't consistently predict when we will stop and we can't stay stopped. Every addict stops bingeing from time to time. We have to. We run out of food, time and privacy. This forces us to stop. It is staying stopped that constitutes recovery. Recovery is long-term commitment to a plan of action which includes abstinence from bingeing and from our addictive substances.

Why a Weighed and Measured Food Plan?

The next chapter will discuss in detail the recovery food plan. But first it might be helpful to address the question of why a food plan is necessary. Why weigh and measure our food? There are so many rationalizations as to why not to weigh and measure (and I won't even enumerate the excuses), that it seems appropriate and helpful to outline the reasons why we do such a thing. Indeed, why a food plan at all?

The first half of the First Step says, "We admitted we were powerless over food." This is the physical manifestation of the disease. And because we are powerless over food, "our lives had become unmanageable." Of course, we are not powerless over every form of food, so it is the job of the food plan to be our guideline in the elimination of those foods which trigger addiction. This is a physical phenomenon. The food plan is a guide to physical recovery. It clearly defines what to eat and what to avoid. This is where honesty begins. When we get honest about our food, it opens the way to honesty in other areas of our life.

All food addicts identify with volume eating, binge eating, gorging and overeating. Weighing and measuring are methods of managing volume. In recovery, we weigh our food instead of our bodies! The cup and scale establish boundaries for our food. In the disease process, the eating experience has been virtually limitless. Our eating was curtailed only by physical, social or financial limitations. In recovery, we manage food intake by use of the cup and the scale. This discipline creates a boundary for that which has been without boundaries.

We abstain from that "first bite." We abstain from the first compulsive bite, the first spontaneous bite, the first addictive bite and the first extra bite. Compulsive eating entails eating over feelings. When we experience toxic feelings, it is an addictive response to reach for food to soothe those feelings. In recovery, we learn alternatives to "eating over it." Spontaneous eating is the hallmark of the undisciplined will. No more do "I eat what I want when I want it!" Taking the extra bite is illustrated by picking up that extra green bean. It is not the bean that is the problem, but the decision to eat the bean—which indicates that we have taken back our will. All of these destructive patterns will lead back to volume eating and the active disease of addiction.

A food plan offers the joy of guilt-free eating. Guilty eating is one of the major signs of food addiction. Guilt-free eating on the plan is a blessing of recovery. No more punishing self-talk, no more agonizing decisions about food, no more internal debates. Plan, report, commit to your food and let go. Serenity in relation to food is the gift of our food plan in recovery.

A grateful recovering food addict says, "I resisted a weighed and measured food plan for four years. I was working a Twelve-Step program and defining my own abstinence, which of course changed at will. I was not overweight but frequently binged on fruit and other foods which were on the food plan. I purged through exercise. I was unwilling to surrender. I am grateful that I finally hit bottom. I had the constant thought that I could have a small portion of fruit and then would pick at it from three until dinner. Then I couldn't eat a balanced dinner because I had to make up for the fruit. It took getting an online sponsor for me to finally become honest with someone about this. I guess it was easier than doing it face to face. She suggested I might be getting a lot of trigger substances without knowing it and suggested that I read *Food Addiction: The Body Knows*. I have been abstinent ever since and free of cravings. But it took hitting bottom before I was willing to surrender my food plan to someone else and weigh and measure. I got too tired of the hopelessness and the feelings of failure. I was lucky that I did not have withdrawal. I was on a pink cloud for those early weeks. The gifts I have received are beyond description, such as being free of cravings and decisions about food. Now my clothes fit the same way every day. Best of all, I am more even-tempered and more patient with my family. These all are truly the gifts received from abstinence."

Goals of the Food Plan

Eliminate all addictive substances.

Balance protein and carbohydrate consumption.

Manage volume.

Provide good nutrition.

Provide regular distribution of nutrients through the day to maintain a level metabolism.

6

Getting Clean on the Recovery Food Plan

Abstinence

One of the greatest struggles in recovery is defining abstinence, which is a must for reaching and maintaining physical recovery. Some who have difficulty staying abstinent never get physically clean. When a food addict ingests even a small amount of an addictive substance, cravings are triggered and along with them the urge to binge.

It has become popular to use an abbreviated (no sugar, flour, wheat) definition of abstinence. There is a problem with this abbreviation. We could abstain from sugar, flour and wheat for the rest of our lives and continue to stay in the disease forever by eating high-fat foods, volume and refined carbohydrate snacks. We could eat them all day and all night and still say that we are abstinent. We could show up at meetings and claim to be abstinent right after a huge binge. This definition is just too limited. Abstinence needs to be defined as abstinence from all addictive foods and behaviors, including personal binge foods and volume, plus a commitment to a weighed and measured food plan.

Begin to work the food plan right away. Take it one meal at a time. Do not wait until Monday, tomorrow morning or January first to begin abstinence. Do it now! In order to get clean and stay that way, a food addict needs to follow this list of practices:

Read the list of ingredients for every food purchase.
Know all of the names for sugar; many are hidden.
Understand the zero-sugar concept.

Get the recipe or ingredients for mixtures ordered in restaurants.

Mistrust sugar-free labels on foods.

Avoid mixtures of food prepared by others.

Eat simply.

Be prepared by planning ahead.

Take responsibility for all food eaten.

Leave nothing to chance.

This kind of informed eating results in relief from cravings. When struggling with abstinence, check sweeteners. Many contain dextrose, and all of the packets contain enough sugar to trigger craving. Zero sugar is the goal, but sugar is not the only substance which will trigger the addictive process. Review and eliminate the following foods which result in an addictive response:

Alcoholic beverages and extracts

Chocolate

Flour

High-fat foods

Personal trigger foods

Puffed or popped grains

Refined and processed food

Sugar

Volume eating

Wheat

Because we deserve clean abstinence, we need to examine the ingredients list of every food we eat; eliminate all foods that contain addictive substances; and identify changes we will to make in order to achieve and maintain physical abstinence. We no longer browse for substitutes! The "substitute browser" can be found in the grocery and health food store looking for "abstinent" forms of pasta, ice cream, candy, cake, crackers and bread in an attempt to maintain old eating patterns developed in the disease. The commitment to abstinence-based recovery involves surrender to the fact that these foods cannot be tolerated physically because they are not sugar-free or flour-free. Despite their appearance as health, diet or sugarless foods, they contain flour and other refined carbohydrates which will trigger the disease.

Longing for the old way of eating takes us mentally back into the disease process and often leads to relapse. A new way of thinking–recovery thinking–involves designing a new way of eating without the addictive foods we have come to depend upon. Seeking and preparing appropriate high-quality foods is challenging, exciting and supports our recovery process. We eat differently now because our energy is directed toward recovery. We no longer manipulate our food plan in order to maintain the old way of eating. We never shop for trouble! We appreciate our food plan and enjoy clean abstinence. Richard sums up this approach when he says, "I strive for effortless abstinence; it is what I am, what I do and it is as much a part of me as breathing out and breathing in."

Recovery Food Plan

Here is the most up-to-date food plan formulated for food addiction recovery. Be sure you review this revised version even if you are an experienced user of the food plan. You may discover that there are new refinements. This plan is based on the concept of abstinence from all foods which will trigger cravings. Abstinence is the foundation of recovery upon which physical, emotional and spiritual growth is built.

Before using this or any other food plan, be sure to check with your doctor for approval.

Daily Portions

Breakfast
One fruit
One protein
One dairy
One grain

Lunch/Dinner
One protein
One raw vegetable
One cooked vegetable
One starch or grain

Before Bed
One fruit
One dairy

Daily
One fat

Daily Options
Spice, one tablespoon
Sugar-free condiments,
  two tablespoons
Sweeteners, six servings*
Sugar-free broth, one cup

WOMEN'S PORTION SIZES
Protein: four ounces (two eggs)
Starch: one cup (eight ounces potato)
Vegetable: (one cup)
Fruit: six ounces

*Note: Exclude sweeteners which contain dextrose, maltodextrose or poly-dextrose. This includes all packets. Saccharin and liquid saccharin can be used with this plan. Read the warning on the label.

Dairy: one cup
Cottage cheese: one-half cup
Fat: one tablespoon or three teaspoons

MEN'S PORTION SIZES

Protein: six ounces (three eggs)
Starch: one cup (eight ounces potato)
Vegetable: one cup
Fruit: six ounces
Dairy: one cup
Cottage cheese: one-half cup
Fat: two tablespoons or six teaspoons

Maintenance

Most people maintain on the original food plan. If weight loss is too rapid or too extreme, adjust the food plan with the help of an individual experienced in its use and familiar with the recovery formula of the food plan. The most common error made when making additions to the plan involves adding extra dairy and fruit. Since these are high-sugar foods, their addition negatively affects the carbohydrate-protein balance by increasing the sugar content of the food plan. Make additions, one per week, taking at least three weeks to complete the changes, in the following manner:

1. Add one teaspoon of oil to each meal, equaling one additional tablespoon per day.
2. Add one ounce of protein to each meal.
3. Add two ounces of complex carbohydrate (grain or starchy vegetable) to each meal.

Abstinent Food List

PROTEIN—FOUR OUNCES FOR WOMEN, SIX OUNCES FOR MEN, EXCEPTIONS NOTED

Beef (five ounces for men)

Chicken

Cooked beans/legumes
(one cup for women, one
and a half cups for men)

Eggs (two large for women,
three large for men)

Fish

Lamb

Pork

Shellfish

Tempeh

Tofu (eight ounces for
women, twelve ounces
for men)

Turkey

Veal

VEGETABLES—ONE SERVING EQUALS ONE CUP

Artichokes (not marinated
in oil)

Asparagus

Bamboo shoots

Beans (green and yellow)

Beets

Bok choy

Broccoli

Brussels sprouts

Cabbage

Carrots

Cauliflower

Celery

Chinese cabbage

Cucumber

Eggplant

Endive

Escarole

Lettuce

Mushrooms

Okra

Onions

Parsley

Peppers

Pickles, dill

Pimentos

Radishes

Romaine lettuce

VEGETABLES—ONE SERVING EQUALS ONE CUP *(continued)*

Rutabaga
Sauerkraut
Snowpeas
Spinach
Sprouts
Summer squash

Tomatoes
Turnips
Water chestnuts
Watercress
Zucchini

FRUIT—ONE SERVING EQUALS SIX OUNCES

Apple
Apricot
Berries
Cantaloupe
Cranberries
Grapefruit
Honeydew
Kiwi
Lemon, lime

Nectarine
Orange
Peach
Pear
Pineapple
Plum
Rhubarb
Tangerine
Watermelon

STARCHES—ONE SERVING EQUALS ONE CUP

All starchy beans and legumes
Acorn, butternut or spaghetti squash, winter squash
Green peas
Potato (eight ounces scale weight)
Yams and sweet potato (eight ounces scale weight)

WHOLE GRAINS

Barley
Brown rice and brown basmati rice
Buckwheat
Oat bran
Oatmeal

GRAINS *(continued)*

Millet   Steel cut oats

Quinoa   Teff

Rye   Whole oats

FAT—DAILY SERVING EQUALS ONE TABLESPOON PER DAY

Canola oil   Olive oil

Other oils are acceptable, but we favor olive and canola.

Trigger Foods

We abstain from all forms of alcohol, cocoa, chocolate, caffeine, and sweetened products including gum, desserts, yogurt, cough drops, cough syrup and candy. This category includes regular sweeteners and artificial sweeteners.

Sugar: We abstain from sugar in all forms. Refer to Appendix I to review all of the names of sugar. A good rule of thumb is to discard any product that contains ingredients with obscure names, even if that product is labeled sugar-free.

Flour: We abstain from all forms of flour such as corn and cornmeal, wheat, rice, barley, rye and products such as corn chips and tacos. We abstain from starches such as corn starch and arrowroot.

Wheat: We abstain from all wheat products, including macaroni, noodles, bread, pizza, crackers, pita, bagels, muffins, shredded wheat, whole grain wheat, wheat flour and modified food starch.

High-fat foods: We abstain from all high-fat foods, including fried food, butter, sour cream, cream cheese, dairy products over 2 percent fat, hard cheese, ricotta cheese, nuts and seeds. Beware of high-fat processed meat products such as hot dogs, ham, bacon and sausage. Even if they are sugar-free, they contain too much fat and too little protein. These processed meats are often 80 to 90 percent fat. To check the fat content of such products, calculate the percentage of fat. For instance, if there are one hundred sixty calories per serving and one hundred twenty calories of fat per serving, one hundred twenty over one hundred sixty equals three-fourths. Therefore the product is 75 percent fat. This would not be a protein product, but an animal fat product unfit for the food plan.

High-sugar fruits: We abstain from high-sugar fruits, including dried fruit, bananas, grapes, cherries, fruit juice, mangos, raisins and high-fat avocados.

Puffed and popped grains: We abstain from puffed and popped grains such as popped corn and puffed cereals. Puffing and popping refines the product. Refinement produces addictive substances.

Recovery Food Plan Guidelines

• Prepare food by baking, boiling, grilling, broiling, steaming and stir-frying in cooking spray. Be sure the spray is alcohol-free. We do not use our oil portion for frying.

• Beware of nonfat and low-fat food. Many times when fat content goes down, starches and sugars replace it. Check the ingredients carefully; they may contain trigger substances.

• Schedule meals approximately four to five hours apart to maintain level metabolism.

• Use a variety of foods in order to avoid boredom. Using a single food frequently may indicate that it is a trigger food. It is very important to vary food.

• Eliminate caffeine, an addictive substance that stimulates appetite.

• Limit red meat (beef, veal, pork) to three times per week.

• Limit eggs to four per week, or use egg whites to reduce cholesterol.

• Iodized salt contains sugar, which keeps the iodine in suspension. Look for salt without iodine as a sugar-free choice. Assume restaurant salt contains iodine and sugar. Be sure to find and use an iodine supplement.

• Check labels on all meat products for added sugar. You may be surprised to find that dextrose is added to frozen turkeys. All deli meat contains sugar and starch.

• Diet soda is a trigger due to the caramel color, which is made from sugar. Some diet sodas now contain sugar, and others with "natural flavors" may contain sugar.

• Make water your drink of choice. It is the fluid your body needs. Adequate hydration supports abstinence and good health.

• Avoid extreme exercise programs. The food plan supports a maximum of about forty-five munutes of exercise a day.

• Use a multivitamin and mineral supplement daily. Good nutrition supports abstinence.

• It is acceptable to have two cooked vegetables at one meal and two raw vegetables at the other. For instance, have a two-cup salad for lunch and two cups of cooked vegetables for dinner.

• Distribute fat throughout the day by eating one teaspoon at each meal. We prefer high-quality olive and canola oils. Avoid hydrogenated and saturated fats, your body cannot utilize them. Margarine is not a healthful choice, due to trans-fatty acids.

• Avoid fruit juice due to the simple sugar content. Juicing eliminates the fiber we need to satisfy our hunger, leaving only liquid and sugar. Juice is a highly processed food which we eliminate. Choose whole fruit, which is more slowly digested and absorbed. Weigh fruit after it is peeled and cored.

• Dairy products are not recommended for protein substitution because they deliver too much carbohydrate and too little protein and calories, leading to increased hunger. Many adults suffer from lactose intolerance. If you have this condition, substitute two ounces of protein for dairy or use two tablespoons of high-protein powder. Some lactose intolerant individuals can tolerate yogurt and Lactaid milk. Beware of Lactaid pills, they contain sugar.

• Measure tofu before cooking; eight ounces for women and twelve ounces for men. All other foods are weighed after cooking.

Watch Out for Sweeteners

Let's talk about artificially sweetened products, including soda, gum, liquids, pills and packets. Although they are not to be considered a healthy choice, the only sweeteners appropriate for the food plan are saccharin tablets and liquid saccharin sweetener. These are non-nutritive products. Non-nutritive means that the sweetener has no nutritional value and therefore contains no sugar or carbohydrate, which provide calories and trigger addiction. The federal government has eliminated saccharin from its list of cancer-causing chemicals. All of the packets of powdered sweeteners are nutritive, that is, they contain some form of sugar which will trigger the addictive process.

Beware of all other nutritive sweeteners if they are highly refined carbohydrates. Refined carbohydrate is the food addict's drug of choice. Limit artificial sweeteners to six or fewer per day. Our experiences with chewing gum include obsession, compulsion and withdrawal symptoms. It is important to realize that so-called sugar-free gum contains sugars including mannitol, sorbitol and glucose syrup. Read labels and think twice before introducing these forms of sugar into your system. Stevia triggers cravings due to the dextrose that is used in processing both the powdered and liquid forms. Fruit juice sweeteners and rice syrup are disguised sugar and not appropriate for our food plan.

All About Protein and Carbohydrates

The protein included in the food plan is favorable to the brain chemistry of the food addict. Have you ever noticed that when you eat high-carbohydrate, low-protein meals, you react by feeling drowsy? Combining protein with carbohydrate makes the food plan work because protein limits serotonin production by those high-carbohydrate foods. Brain serotonin is the food addict's "drug of choice." Carbohydrates are the most effective precursor of brain serotonin. They flood the brain with this chemical, which acts as a painkiller and a tranquilizer. Since protein moderates the production of brain serotonin when it is combined with carbohydrate, it is vital to a successful food plan. It is important to remember that the balance of high-protein foods with high-carbohydrate foods makes this food plan work. Use beans for protein no more than one time per day. Otherwise your food plan will be too high in carbohydrate, and the protein-carbohydrate balance will be disturbed.

Weighing and Measuring

The best way to manage volume and to stay within the boundaries of the food plan is to weigh and measure food. We have found that the "eyeball method" of measuring our food is inexact at best and often guided by our disease. As Maria says, "My eyeballs are compulsive overeaters!" True freedom from overeating, binge eating or undereating can be achieved by the use of a reliable little scale. It removes all self-will and self-doubt. The digital scales (when they are working properly) are very accurate, weighing right to the exact tenth of an ounce.

Weighing and measuring both at home and away from home is heartily recommended by those who practice diligence in recovery. Little scales carried in purse or pocket have become commonplace among recovering people. When one strays from the use of the scale and measuring cups and spoons, there is often a slide into overeating grains, fruit and fat. Cups, scales and measuring spoons provide a way to manage volume. All food except tofu is weighed and measured after it is cooked. If any part of a food, such as a peel, is to be discarded, weigh the edible part only.

The cup and scale keep us honest. When we weigh and measure our food, we do not have to worry about weighing ourselves. We weigh our bodies no more than once a month. On maintenance, it may be necessary to weigh once a week. This is a trust issue. We learn to trust the measurements of the food plan. We no longer have to jump on the scale each morning. In fact, that is the difference–in recovery we weigh our food, not our bodies.

Menu and Recipe Ideas

To help you get started, here are meal suggestions for a week with recipes (for those dishes marked with an asterisk), preparation suggestions and recovery hints. These recipes use women's protein portions. Men need to make appropriate adjustments.

Sunday

BREAKFAST:	Blueberry Muffins*
LUNCH:	Chili*
DINNER:	Tuna Cole Slaw with Frozen Peas*
BEFORE BED:	Yogurt and Fresh Pineapple

Monday

BREAKFAST: Pancake with Yogurt and Strawberries*
LUNCH: Italian Casserole*
DINNER: Chicken, Salad, Baked Sweet Potato
BEFORE BED: Fruit Shake with Nonfat Milk and
              Peaches*

Tuesday

BREAKFAST: Homemade Turkey Sausage*, Hash Brown
              Potatoes*, Grapefruit, Milk
LUNCH: Mexican Salad*
DINNER: Hamburger-Cabbage Soup*
BEFORE BED: Cottage Cheese and Hot Blueberries

Wednesday

BREAKFAST: Oatmeal, Tofu, Apple and Yogurt*
LUNCH: Oriental Soup*
DINNER: Baked Fish, Baked Potato, Double Salad
BEFORE BED: Baked Apple*, Buttermilk

Thursday

BREAKFAST: Apple and Butternut Squash Bake*
LUNCH: Onion and Tuna Stir-Fry*, Mixed Raw
              Vegetable
DINNER: Turkey, Squash, Beets, Salad
BEFORE BED: Leftover Turkey, Melon

Friday
  BREAKFAST: Rye Cereal, Milk, Orange, Turkey Sausage
  LUNCH: Ratatouille and Chicken over Baked
                Potato*
  DINNER: Black Beans and Brown Rice, Double
                Salad
  BEFORE BED: Mixed Berries and Cottage Cheese

Saturday
  BREAKFAST: Margot's Mush*
  LUNCH: Potato Salad on Greens*
  DINNER: Chargrilled Fish, Baked Potato, Double
                Salad (Eating Out)
  BEFORE BED: Soy Milk and Strawberry Shake*

Blueberry Muffins

2 eggs   ½ cup dry oat bran
⅓ cup powdered milk   ¼ teaspoon cinnamon
6 ounces blueberries

Preheat oven to 350°F. In a small bowl, beat the eggs well. Add the remaining ingredients to the eggs and stir until blended. Pour mixture into muffin tins sprayed with alcohol-free cooking spray. Fill each tin ¾ full. Bake the muffins for 20 minutes or until firm to the touch. Allow muffins to cool for 5 minutes.

This recipe is the equivalent of one complete breakfast for women; men should make the protein adjustment.

Food Plan Equivalent: *1 Protein, 1 Dairy, 1 Grain, 1 Fruit,*
¼ Teaspoon Seasoning

Chili

1 cup cooked kidney beans or pinto beans	1½ cups sugar-free tomato juice
4 ounces (men 6 ounces) lean hamburger, cooked and drained of fat	1 tablespoon salsa
	1 teaspoon chili powder
	1 teaspoon cumin
¼ cup diced onions	Dash hot sauce
¼ cup diced peppers	

Note: Choose the leanest hamburger available, preferably less than 5 percent fat. If the hamburger appears to be fatty, rinse it under warm water and then measure.

Combine all ingredients in a soup pot and cook for one-half hour on low heat until the vegetables are tender.

This recipe is the equivalent of a complete lunch or dinner. Since it contains two cups of cooked vegetables, it should be served on a day when the other meal is comprised of two cups of raw vegetables.

Food Plan Equivalent: *1 Protein, 1 Starch, 2 Cooked Vegetables, 1 Tablespoon Sauce, 2 Teaspoons Seasoning*

Tuna Cole Slaw

4 ounces water-packed, low-sodium canned tuna	1 tablespoon sugar-free mayonnaise (see recipe to follow)
1½ cups shredded cabbage	2 tablespoons plain, sugar-free, nonfat yogurt
¼ cup shredded carrot	
¼ cup diced onion	Dash vinegar
1 cup frozen baby green peas	Dash celery salt
	Dash garlic powder

Note: Look for low-sodium, water-packed tuna to avoid the additives in regular tuna.

In a small bowl, mix the tuna, vegetables and frozen peas. (Do not defrost peas.) In a separate container, mix the mayonnaise, yogurt, vinegar, celery salt and garlic powder until blended. Toss the tuna mixture with the mayonnaise until well combined.

This is a complete dinner or lunch for one.

Homemade Sugar-Free Mayonnaise

2 eggs
2 tablespoons lemon juice
Dash salt

1 teaspoon dry mustard
1¼ cups oil

Combine the eggs, lemon juice, salt and dry mustard in a blender. Blend on high speed for 1 minute. Slowly add the oil and blend until well mixed. The result will be delicious sugar-free mayo.

Food Plan Equivalent: *1 Protein, 1 Fat, 1 Starch, 2 Raw Vegetables, 1 Condiment, 1 Seasoning*

Breakfast Pancake with Yogurt and Strawberries

2 eggs, beaten
½ cup of any mixed uncooked grains (oat bran, oatmeal, quinoa flakes, cream of buckwheat and rye cereal)
1 tablespoon water

Dash cinnamon
1 ounce sugar-free applesauce
1 cup plain, sugar-free nonfat yogurt
5 ounces strawberries

Note: The grains should be cooked, single-grain cereals, not cold cereals.

Heat a frypan sprayed with alcohol-free cooking spray. In a small bowl, mix the grains, eggs, water, cinnamon and applesauce to form a smooth batter. Pour the batter into the frypan using all of the mixture to make one pancake. Cook the pancake on medium heat until browned on both sides and firm in the center. Top with the yogurt and strawberry mixture and serve.

Food Plan Equivalent: *1 Protein, 1 Dairy, 1 Grain, 1 Fruit*

Italian Casserole

1 cup cooked brown rice
1 egg, beaten
½ teaspoon Italian seasoning
½ teaspoon garlic powder

4 ounces tofu, crumbled
  (6 ounces for men)
1 cup sugar-free pizza sauce
1 cup frozen pepper and
  onion mix, sautéed

Note: There are several brands of sugar-free pizza sauce. Avoid those with "natural flavors," although "natural garlic flavor" is acceptable.

Preheat oven to 400°F. In a medium bowl, blend the rice with the egg and seasonings. Spray an 8-inch pie plate with alcohol-free cooking spray. Pat the rice mixture into the pie plate to form a crust. Bake until firm (8 to 10 minutes). Remove the baked rice crust from the oven; add the crumbled tofu and pizza sauce and blend with the peppers and onions. Bake the casserole until it bubbles around the edges (approximately 5 minutes.)

Food Plan Equivalent: *1 Protein, 1 Grain, 2 Cooked Vegetables,*
1 Teaspoon Seasoning

Peach Shake

1 cup frozen sugar-free   1 cup nonfat milk
   peaches
¼ teaspoon ground nutmeg

Place all ingredients into a blender and blend until smooth.

Food Plan Equivalent: *1 Dairy, 1 Fruit, 1 Spice*

Turkey Sausage

1 pound lean ground turkey   1 tablespoon garlic powder
   meat   1 tablespoon poultry
1 tablespoon ground fennel   seasoning

In a small bowl, combine the turkey and the seasonings. Form the mixture into patties and cook them in a sauté pan for 8 to 10 minutes, or heat the oven to 375°F and bake the patties on a baking pan for 10 minutes or until done. Divide the patties into 4-ounce servings for women or 6-ounce servings for men. Freeze any leftover meat for future use.

Food Plan Equivalent: *1 Protein, 1 Seasoning*

Hash Brown Potatoes - - - - - - - -┐

10 ounces small red potatoes   ⅛ teaspoon salt
½ cup chopped onion   ⅛ teaspoon pepper

Wash the potatoes and poke them with a fork. Microwave the potatoes for approximately 5 minutes until they are cooked, then chop them into bite-sized cubes. Spray a frypan with alcohol-free cooking spray, add chopped potatoes and onion, and stir-fry until browned. Sprinkle with salt and pepper and serve.

Food Plan Equivalent: *1 Condiment, 1 Starch, ¼ Teaspoon Spice*

Mexican Salad - - - - - - - - - ┐

4 ounces lean hamburger, cooked, drained of fat and crumbled
½ teaspoon chili powder
1 cup fat-free refried beans

1 ounce sugar-free salsa
2 cups assorted salad greens, with tomatoes and chopped onions
1 tablespoon sugar-free oil and vinegar dressing

Note: You may toss the assorted salad greens with the vinegar and oil dressing, or you can wait and drizzle the dressing on top of the salsa.

Season the cooked hamburger with chili powder. Cook the refried beans on low heat until warm. On a serving plate, layer the salad greens, the heated refried beans and then the hamburger; top with the salsa.

Food Plan Equivalent: *1 Protein, 1 Starch, 2 Raw Vegetables, ½ Teaspoon Seasoning, 1 Tablespoon Oil*

Hamburger-Cabbage Soup

1 cup cooked shredded
   cabbage
1 cup red kidney beans
1 cup sugar-free tomato juice
1 cup beef broth

4 ounces lean hamburger,
   cooked, drained of fat and
   crumbled
3 cloves
Dash of garlic powder

Mix all ingredients together in a medium-sized soup pot and simmer until the soup thickens slightly.

Food Plan Equivalent: *1 Protein, 1 Starch, 2 Cooked Vegetables,*
1 Broth, 1 Seasoning

Apple, Oats, Tofu and Yogurt

1 cup plain, sugar-free, nonfat
   yogurt
½ cup dry oatmeal

6 ounces chopped apple
½ teaspoon cinnamon
8 ounces tofu

Mix all ingredients in a small bowl until well blended. Serve chilled.

Food Plan Equivalent: *1 Protein, 1 Dairy, 1 Grain, 1 Fruit, 1 Seasoning*

Oriental Soup ------------

4 ounces cooked chicken, diced

2 cups frozen broccoli, carrot, water chestnut mix

1 cup cooked brown rice

1 tablespoon alcohol- and wheat-free tamari sauce

1 cup chicken broth

½ teaspoon garlic powder

Place all ingredients in a soup pot, and cook over medium heat to blend flavors. Serve steaming hot.

Food Plan Equivalent: *1 Protein, 1 Starch, 2 Cooked Vegetables, 1 Broth, Condiment, Seasoning, ½ Teaspoon Spice*

Baked Apple -------------

1 apple, sliced

1 teaspoon cinnamon

1 tablespoon water

Sweetener (optional)

Place apple slices in a small microwavable bowl. Add the water and cinnamon to the apples, and microwave for about 2 to 3 minutes on high power until tender. **Note:** If using sweetener, use liquid saccharin or saccharin tablets only since packet sweeteners contain sugar.

Food Plan Equivalent: *1 Fruit, 1 Seasoning*

Apple and Butternut Squash Bake

4 ounces cooked chicken	1 cup cubed cooked butternut
1 cup diced apple	squash
⅓ cup nonfat powdered milk	½ teaspoon cinnamon

Preheat oven to 375°F. Spray a small glass dish with cooking spray, and place chicken and diced apple in the dish. In a small bowl, combine the powdered milk and squash. Spread the squash mixture over the chicken and sprinkle with cinnamon. Bake for 15 to 20 minutes.

This is a delicious complete breakfast using unusual ingredients.

Food Plan Equivalent: *1 Protein, 1 Dairy, 1 Starch, 1 Fruit,*
1 Teaspoon Seasoning

Onion and Tuna Stir-Fry

1 cup cooked sliced onion	1 tablespoon alcohol- and
4 ounces water-packed, low-	wheat-free tamari sauce
sodium canned tuna	1½ teaspoons roasted
1 cup cooked brown rice	sesame oil

Spray a sauté pan with alcohol-free cooking spray and heat. Sauté onions until they are tender. Add the tuna to the pan and sauté until browned; add the brown rice and cook until heated through. Transfer to a serving dish. Toss the onion and tuna stir-fry with the tamari sauce and the sesame oil and serve.

Food Plan Equivalent: *1 Protein, 1 Grain, 1 Cooked Vegetable,*
Condiment, ½ Oil

Ratatouille

2 large onions, diced
2 cups diced red, yellow,
    green peppers
2 minced garlic cloves
4 zucchini, diced

4 yellow squash, diced
1 eggplant, diced
1 can diced tomatoes
2 tablespoons Italian
    seasoning

Sauté onions, peppers and garlic in a skillet sprayed with alcohol-free cooking spray, and cook until tender. Transfer the ingredients to a large soup pot, and add remaining ingredients. Simmer on low heat for one hour, or until the vegetables are tender.

Note: For a complete meal, add 4 ounces of cooked, cubed chicken to 2 cups of the cooked ratatouille and serve over an 8-ounce baked potato or 1 cup steamed brown rice.

Food Plan Equivalent: *1 Cup Equals 1 Cooked Vegetable, 2 Seasonings*

Margot's Mush

2 eggs
6 ounces frozen mixed
    berries without sugar
    added

½ cup dry oatmeal
1 teaspoon cinnamon
1 cup plain, sugar-free,
    nonfat yogurt

In a small microwavable bowl, mix the eggs, frozen berries, oatmeal and cinnamon. Microwave for 2 minutes on high. Stir and microwave for an additional two minutes. Fold in one cup of yogurt and serve. This is a fast and delicious breakfast.

Food Plan Equivalent: *1 Protein, 1 Dairy, 1 Grain, 1 Fruit, 1 Teaspoon Seasoning*

Potato Salad

8 ounces red potatoes

Dressing:

2 tablespoons plain sugar-free, nonfat yogurt

1½ tablespoons red wine vinegar

1 tablespoon sugar-free mayonnaise

1 teaspoon yellow mustard

dash garlic powder

1 teaspoon dried parsley

2 hard-boiled eggs, diced

2 cups assorted salad greens

2 tablespoons chopped onion

Cook the potatoes in boiling water until fully cooked but barely tender. Rinse, drain, cool and dice potatoes.

In a small bowl, combine the yogurt, red wine vinegar, mayonnaise, mustard, garlic powder and parsley. Blend well.

Pour the dressing mixture over the potatoes. Add the diced eggs and stir gently until evenly distributed. Serve the chilled potato salad over salad greens. Garnish with chopped onion.

Note: For instructions on how to make a homemade sugar-free mayonnaise, turn to page 106.

Food Plan Equivalent: *1 Protein, 1 Starch, 2 Raw Vegetables, 1 Oil, Condiment, Seasoning*

Strawberry Shake

1 cup frozen strawberries   1 cup soy milk

Place the strawberries and soy milk in a blender, and blend until smooth.

Note: Read the soy milk ingredients carefully. Look for a product containing only soybeans and water. Avoid soy milk products with added sweeteners.

Food Plan Equivalent: *1 Dairy, 1 Fruit*

7

The Twelve Steps: Our Recovery Path

The Twelve Steps are the great gift of recovery that can't be found in any weight-loss program or diet club. They are clear directions designed for addicts. A food plan without the steps is just a diet. Notice the steps are written in the past tense, plural. They are no theory; they have worked for millions. Many people use different recovery groups to learn about the steps—those especially for food addicts as well as open AA meetings. We discuss the steps with our sponsors and at recovery meetings. We use the program literature such as *Alcoholics Anonymous* (the "Big Book") and AA's *Twelve Steps and Twelve Traditions*. Traditionally when using the Big Book we have substituted the words "food addict" for "alcoholic" and "food" for "alcohol." The recovery programs for food addicts have wonderful literature, as well.

The Twelve Steps are a way of life. Every journey begins with the first step! Step One states the problem, Step Two states the solution and Steps Three through Twelve are the method for arriving at the solution. We incorporate the steps into our lives in stages: First, we become familiar with them; next, we do the work by studying and writing. If we persist, the steps become part our lives and are reflected in our values, attitudes, beliefs and conduct. Step Twelve tells us where we are going and what we will be getting—a spiritual experience is the result of these steps, and with it we are relieved of the obsession to eat addictively.

One, Two, Three:
Striving for Balance

Achieving balance in all areas of life–spiritual, physical and psychological–is the foremost challenge of recovery. Try to imagine a three-legged stool. One leg of the stool represents your physical needs, the second leg represents your spiritual needs, the third leg of the stool stands for your psychological needs. In order for the stool to stand upright and balanced, all three legs need to be equal. In early recovery, we work on the area that needs to be addressed first, which is physical recovery in Step One. In Step Two we begin mental recovery, and in Step Three we stabilize spiritually. The first three steps treat all three areas of life. Our stool is more balanced from the very start!

Step One: Identifying the Problem

We admitted we were powerless over food–that our lives had become unmanageable.

In the First Step we come to understand that we are powerless over food and, because of that powerlessness, our lives are unmanageable. It takes time to realize the full extent of the harm caused by addictive food substances and how devastating the addictive process has been. Over time, we learn that we are powerless because our bodies cannot handle certain food substances. We are powerless when we add addictive substance to these bodies which cannot tolerate them. Addictive foods don't cause us any trouble when we leave them in the grocery store. It is only when we ingest them that the addiction is triggered. Whatever changes brain chemistry and alters mood is addictive! Food fits that bill.

In Step One we begin our physical recovery. We start recovery by reviewing the course of our food addiction. The fact that we are powerless has been established each time we eat in an addictive way. We need to acknowledge that our body chemistry is different from those who are not addicted. The first bite of trigger food sets up the craving phenomenon. Eating addictive food triggers loss of control. After eating it, we cannot predict how much we will eat or how we will behave. The food addict lives in compulsive slavery. Existence under such circumstances makes life unmanageable.

Every food addict has at some time had the fantasy that control and enjoyment of addictive foods can be regained. The person who has become addicted to food cannot return to controlled eating. We have a serious disease against which our physical and mental resistance has no power. The disease of food addiction is progressive and incurable. It has been proven that this baffling disease can be arrested at any point in its progression if the addict is willing to accept help. The first step in recovery is to completely acknowledge that we are food addicts and cannot afford to take even one bite of trigger food.

It is one thing to know intellectually that we have a problem with food. It is another to accept at a deep emotional level the concept that we are powerless to control what we eat. For most of us, gut-level acceptance of this fact comes only after repeated failure to prove that we can achieve control and again be "normal." We must come to understand that this is not a question of willpower. Obsession and compulsion are not rational, therefore this cannot be an issue of willpower. This is an issue of compulsion which pushes us from bite to bite through each binge. Trying to use self-will to control compulsion is like trying to put out a fire with gasoline. Once we take the first bite, determination shifts and fuels the compulsion to eat more of everything. Despite our strongest resolution to stop binge eating, we continue.

If we persist in the belief that we can safely take that first bite, that we can control the intake of binge food despite the fact that we have proved over and over again that we cannot control it, then we are no longer rationally dealing with food. The same behavior always brings the same results. If we pick up the first bite of addictive food, we can expect to binge. When we rationalize (believe the lies the disease tells us), we are not being rational. The first bite eventually equals a binge for us every time. No matter what mental gymnastics we perform, the body will always react to binge food in the same manner. The food will trigger the compulsive use of more. At that point, we are back into the vicious cycle of obsession and compulsion—powerlessness and unmanageability.

This is the surrender step. We surrender to the fact that use of addictive foods will always result in loss of control. We have lost control over food and our lives. Acceptance of this step paves the way to recovery. As we grow to understand our own powerlessness and how unmanageable our lives have become, we begin to understand the power addiction has over our lives. We start our recovery by writing the history of our food addiction. We understand that we have an incurable illness and that abstinence is the way to deal with it.

Take some time to think about and write your answers to the following questions:

- What does it mean to me to be powerless over food?
- In what ways is my life unmanageable?
- Have I accepted at a gut level that I am powerless over food—that my life has become unmanageable?
- Do I still reserve the right to eat one addictive bite?
- Do I think that I can take just one small piece of trigger food and stop?
- Do I realize that the use of trigger food will always bring negative results?
- What are the consequences of my use of addictive foods?

Step Two: Finding the Solution

Came to believe that a Power greater than ourselves could restore us to sanity.

The course of this step begins with a belief. Every one of our thoughts and actions begins with a belief, whether toxic or favorable. Before Step Two, we are like the small boy who tried to move a rock from his path. As he kicked at it, pushed and shoved, his father watched from the window. The father went to the boy and said, "Son, why didn't you use all of your power to move that rock?" The boy replied, "I did, I used all my strength." The father responded,

"No—you didn't ask me." The boy's belief changed! His father could help him.

In Step Two we search for the power. In Step One we admitted that we could not manage our own lives. In Step Two we begin to understand that some force greater than our own is able to provide the strength and direction that we need. In this step, we no longer have to preserve the pretense of self-sufficiency. My friend John says, "When we are hungry we get some food, when we are broke we get some money, when we are powerless we get some Power." To do this, an open mind is recommended, along with an attitude of willingness.

We are free to use any conception of a Higher Power that is comfortable or familiar for us. Those who have trouble with the idea of God can relax. For some the Higher Power might be the strength of the group or the strength of the people who have found a solution. Jill's sponsor told her, "Don't worry about praying to God for your abstinence, I will pray every day to my God for you!" She put her faith in her sponsor's prayer and it worked. Every day her sponsor reminded Jill that she had requested abstinence for her. Eventually she found her own Higher Power.

We have admitted our powerlessness. In the Second Step we find power, faith and sanity. Do we doubt the insanity of this disease? We may think: "But I am not really insane." Then let's look at some of the things we did in the disease: hiding food, closet eating, gorging, endangering our health, spending hours obsessing about food and then lying about it. When considering our lives of desperation in the addiction, we strive for sanity because there is nothing appealing about the lies and subterfuge. Willingness to follow the directions of recovering people is the way to sanity.

This Second Step is the beginning of mental recovery. A clue to sane thinking is what we discovered in Step One. We learned that we are powerless over everything except what we think, what we say and what we do. Those are the things we can change. In the disease, we wanted to change the world. This is a major ego issue. If we work to change the world, nothing happens. But when we change ourselves, the world changes. We learn to focus on what it is about our behavior, attitudes and beliefs that gets us into trouble.

In order to live this step, we come to recognize that there is a Power greater than ourselves and that we have a need to be restored to wholeness. When we ask, we turn on a spiritual force that will restore us to rational thinking and behaving—a natural state of wholeness. We who have been fragmented by the disease of addiction begin to be restored to that state of wholeness.

Take some time to think about and write your answers to the following questions:

- Do I believe there is a power greater than myself?
- Have I observed others who practice the steps living a rational way of life?
- Am I willing to trust that other recovering people have found a way that works?
- Am I willing to find a new manager for my life?

Step Three: Making a Decision

Made a decision to turn our lives and our wills over to the care of God as we understood Him.

In Step Two we formed a new belief. In Step Three we make a decision based upon that belief. Step Three is the beginning of our emotional and spiritual recovery. A process of commitment to recovery begins with this step. The Third-Step decision is one we will never want to rescind.

As compulsive people, we want guarantees. But instead we learn from others in recovery what works. We begin to trust a power greater than ourselves instead of food. This is a turn of one hundred eighty degrees for us. Rebellion may get in the way of this step. As an addict, we want what we want when we want it! We want it our way. How can we trust God to do a better job with our lives than we can? We know what we need and want. Then we ask ourselves, how good is the job that we have done in life? In Steps One and Two we made an admission and expressed a belief. In Step Three, we invite God into our lives, believing he has a better way. Some of us have come to know God and still struggle with food. Every day we have a choice of whether to reach for God instead of food. We say: "God's will, not mine be done." Letting go and letting God is the way to peace for the troubled addict.

Take some time to think about and write your answers to the following questions:

- Is dependence on God a source of strength or weakness?
- Do I believe there is another way which is more effective than mine?
- Am I willing to depend on God to help me change my life?

- Can I improve matters using my unaided will?
- Is God working in my sponsor's life?
- Have I become willing to turn my life and my will over to the care of God?
- How will I allow God into my life?

Step Four: Cleaning House

Made a searching and fearless moral inventory of ourselves.

In the first three steps, we begin our physical, psychological and spiritual recovery. The whole person has begun the recovery process, because we are the sum of our physical, psychological and spiritual selves. The wisdom of the steps is that within the first three, the whole person has become better. Now it is time to clean house.

In order to live without resorting to food whenever we are disturbed, we need to analyze what it is about our personalities and our way of reacting to people and events that should be changed. Our old ways have not worked. Very early in life we ate to avoid feeling pain. In this way our addiction caused us to short-circuit the process of growing up. Our goal is to become emotionally and spiritually mature enough to deal with life without overeating. Before we finish Steps Four and Five, we discover how we have been sabotaging ourselves and how we can begin to exchange our liabilities for assets.

We take a moral inventory concerning principles of conduct. We look at the ways we broke our own rules and how addiction to food and other substances caused such a course of behavior. A good inventory includes both assets and liabilities. We wish to include both our strengths and our flaws so we can use those strengths to overcome our weaknesses.

Getting started may seem to be the hardest part. Because this is a written step, not a mental one, we get a legal pad and a good pen and we are ready to go. The next stage is to pray for the courage to overcome the fears that might keep us from honestly looking at the people, places, behaviors, emotions and situations that were part of our addictive process. We need to write about these departments of life: family and social relationships, sex, education, spiritual, work and health. How did addiction affect those areas of life? Next we ask in what ways were we resentful, jealous, afraid, suspicious, inconsiderate, dishonest and selfish. What harm have we done to others? We begin to see the effect of addiction on ourselves and the people with whom we share our lives.

In Step Four we take a searching and fearless moral inventory of ourselves. This is the step where we stop taking the inventory of other people and start taking our own. In this step we move forward into the kind of sane thinking which is suggested in the Serenity Prayer—to change ourselves and to accept others. We learn to focus upon our own shortcomings which can be altered and to stop the judgment, blame and criticism which fed our resentments, guilt and fears. This is where we learn to evaluate and correct our behavior, attitudes and beliefs. After completing the Fourth Step, we experience a great flood of relief. We are not to blame, our family members were not to blame—addiction caused our pain. In addiction we became what we did not want to be, now we have found a way to change.

Take some time to think about and write your answers to the following questions:

- Have I taken a searching inventory, looking at all departments of my life?
- Did shame and fear keep me from looking at painful episodes?
- After completing this step, can I now see that food addiction caused unacceptable and ineffective behaviors that hurt myself and others?
- Has it become harder to justify the next bite of binge food now that I see the effect of food addiction on my behavior?

Step Five: Trusting God and Others

Admitted to God, to ourselves, and to another human being, the exact nature of our wrongs.

Step Five shows us the way to beneficial dependency. We have been in a process of exchanging our unhealthy dependency on substances for dependency on God and healthy people. Some of us thought that independence and self-sufficiency were the way to adult happiness. But imagine life without God and loving people. It would be so cold and lonely. In the Fifth Step, by discussing with God and another human being the exact nature of our wrongs, we begin to examine more openly the truth about our path of addiction. We have been as sick as our secrets. In this step we practice true humility.

Step Five is one which cannot be overlooked. It may not seem important to own up to our destructive beliefs and actions, but it is crucial to continuing recovery. Those who skip the housecleaning are destined to return to addictive eating. We who hated to think we were ever wrong begin to see that the only wrongs that can be corrected are the ones we ourselves have committed. We start this step by admitting to ourselves that we have committed errors which require correction. From there, we admit to our Higher Power that we have now recognized these errors. This is our chance to change our self-destructive patterns. All change begins with recognition, admission and acceptance.

We talk to another human being about the exact nature of our wrongs. This is where we become transparent: hiding, evading, covering up and lying ends here. We find someone with whom we can be open and honest. We choose a sponsor, a clergyman or a therapist—a trusted person whom we can rely upon to keep our discussion confidential and give straightforward feedback. We discuss with him or her all that was revealed in our Fourth Step.

The AA book suggests that when we return home after completing Step Five, we review these five completed steps to determine if anything is missing. Then we thank God "that we know Him better" (*Alcoholics Anonymous*).

Take some time to think about and write your answers to the following questions:

- Have I withheld anything from my Fifth Step?
- Do I now understand the "exact nature of my wrongs"?

- Was I open to the feedback from the person who received my step?
- How do I see things differently now?

Step Six: Ready, Set, Go

Were entirely ready to have God remove all these defects of character.

Step Seven: Humility Is the Key

Humbly asked Him to remove our shortcomings.

We have reviewed Steps One through Five, which are the foundation of change. Here, in the Sixth Step, we begin to change. During the course of addiction we tended to see the pleasure of our defects while ignoring the pain. For instance, when angry we felt self-righteous, powerful and energized, while avoiding looking at how our anger earned us the alienation and contempt of others. During the course of working the recovery steps, while discussing them with someone else, it becomes clear that the consequences of our character defects hurt us. Yet we may be willing to have the most obvious defects removed while clinging to some of our more favored ones. Will we be a zero when we let go of these patterns that make up our personality? They are, after all, a part of us. We pray to be willing to let go. In the Seventh Step, we turn those defects of character over to God. We call upon the grace of God to aid us in releasing our attachment to them. God has been waiting for us to give him our permission for help. When we humbly ask him to remove our shortcomings, we have completed Step Seven.

Take some time to think about and write your answers to the following questions:

- Have I seen how my defects of character hurt me and harmed others?
- Am I willing to give them all over to God?
- Have I given my Higher Power permission to take them away?
- Am I willing to continue releasing my attachment to my character defects?

Step Eight: Willingness to Repair the Damage

Made a list of all persons we had harmed, and became willing to make amends to them all.

Step Nine: Doing the Repair Work

Made direct amends to such people wherever possible, except when to do so would injure them or others.

The first thing we do to complete our amends work is to make a list of those people we have identified in our Fourth Step and discussed in our Fifth Step. The harms we have committed against them stand between us and God. We cannot hope to go further in our spiritual development without making direct amends to those we have hurt. Realizing this, we become willing to make amends to those who are on our list. As in all our steps, if we are not willing, it is time to stop and pray for the willingness. When faith replaces fear, we move ahead, willing to go to any lengths to live a spiritual life.

We prepare our strategy with our sponsor, remembering that the experience is to benefit us spiritually. Our amends will include admissions of wrongdoing followed by changed behavior. For example, repayment of money owed will be arranged, followed by the practice of fiscal responsibility. This is not an apology step, it is the amends step. We make restitution and make up for the harm caused in a substantial way.

It is not advisable to rush to resolution. This is not a step to be performed in early recovery before we are emotionally stable enough to see it through. It will take time, possibly years, to do the work of this step. We start with the people closest to us. Most of us are still loved by family members. We sit down face to face with them and speak frankly, admitting the harm done to them during the course of our active addiction. We then outline the course of action we will take to change our destructive practices. We remember to stay focused on ourselves, avoiding discussion of what others have done. We are cleaning up our side of the street.

After working on our list of family members and close friends, we move on to tougher situations. Working with a sponsor, we refer back to the list of people we have harmed and discuss with our sponsor whether it is time to move on in our amends work. We proceed in the same manner that we employed with our family by admitting our wrongs and describing our plans to change. Continuing to make amends in this manner, we ask for God's guidance and the support of our sponsor when it becomes difficult. We may have a list of persons to whom we refuse to make amends. We pray for willingness to make those amends wherever possible, realizing that we will not complete our amends all at once. The time and place will be revealed in God's time.

Take some time to think about and write your answers to the following questions:

- Have I formulated a list of those who were harmed by my food addiction?
- Am I willing to live a spiritual way of life based on correction of my past errors?
- Have I become willing to make face-to-face amends to all the people on my list?
- Have I begun to make direct amends wherever possible?
- Have I remained willing to complete making amends when the time and place is revealed?
- Are the promises coming true as described in the book *Alcoholics Anonymous*?

Step Ten: Keeping Our House Clean

Continued to take personal inventory and when we were wrong promptly admitted it.

The Tenth Step does not say *if* we were wrong. It says *when* we were wrong, leaving little doubt that we will continue to mess up. This is a program that recognizes progress, not perfection. According to AA literature, there are three types of Step Ten inventory: a spot-check when disturbed, the day's end inventory and an annual review to be shared with our sponsor. Using all three, we discover that the Tenth Step is a powerful tool used to avoid relapse. This inventory gives us the information we need to avoid reverting to those self-destructive patterns that will lead us back into the disease. By taking a daily check, we can determine whether we are moving toward recovery by practicing the steps or moving toward relapse by discarding them. Step Ten is undoubtedly the greatest relapse prevention tool. It is a growth step that, along with Steps Eleven and Twelve, is practiced on a daily basis.

A quick Tenth Step review just before bed might go something like this: What did I do today to weaken my recovery? What did I do today to strengthen my recovery? A more extensive evening inventory might include a checklist. (See Appendix V.) When using this kind of checklist, we include our basic recovery tasks to ensure that we perform them on a scheduled basis. We watch for weaknesses in our recovery program to guard against undermining those actions that support strong recovery. We definitely include on our checklist our persistent defects and behaviors such as gossip, pride, anger, jealousy or fear. It may also be helpful to include honesty in weighing and measuring, planning, and reporting our food. Step Ten is the continued practice of Steps Four through Nine. We watch for our character flaws to resurface and continue to identify them and their consequences. We promptly admit these to another recovering person, usually our sponsor. When times are difficult we increase meetings, pray for help and use our recovery techniques.

Take some time to think about and write your answers to the following questions:

- When problems occur, do I promptly acknowledge that something is wrong and take action to correct it?
- Have I learned to resolve problems without eating over them?
- Do I use my inventory to review my recovery program for strengths and weaknesses?
- What tools do I use to resolve toxic thoughts and feelings?
- Have I made use of "on the spot," "daily" and "annual" inventories?

Step Eleven: Doing the Next Right Thing

Sought through prayer and meditation to improve our conscious contact with God as we understood Him, praying only for knowledge for His will for us and the power to carry that out.

As we have progressed through the steps, we have examined and sought to change toxic attitudes, feelings and beliefs. We have begun to experience a change of personality. In Step Eleven we fill the void created by the elimination of our old ideas and actions with conscious contact with the God of our understanding. We begin to practice the presence of God. The decision we made in Step Three is fulfilled in Step Eleven. We do this through prayer and meditation, which are our means of reaching God.

We heard at meetings that prayer is speaking to God and meditation is listening. We determine the form of meditation we choose to practice and begin to benefit physically, psychologically and spiritually. Regular meditation practiced twice daily is like paying the premiums on our spiritual insurance policy. The great benefits of this practice are not always immediately apparent. Meditation results in deep relaxation that allows for the release of stored-up stress and allows us to move into the future free of old stressors. It provides spiritual, psychological and physical rewards.

Prayer is the other powerful tool in our recovery tool bag. The AA book suggests that we pray in the morning and evening. Wasn't that what our parents and pastors told us in childhood? In the morning we place our lives in God's care, asking for direction and enlightenment. In the evening, after reviewing our day, we ask forgiveness and guidance to correct our errors of the day. What a change this is for us! We give up rationalization and justification of our unacceptable behaviors and ask to be shown how to take corrective actions. When asking for forgiveness for ourselves, we forgive others for perceived harms. The review of our day continues with gratitude for the goodness and the gifts that filled our hours. Spiritual practices often include reading an inspirational thought for the day. A morning started with prayer, meditation and inspirational reading is time well spent for a good daily start. Through the practice of this step, we gain the strength and courage to carry out God's will for us on a daily basis.

Take some time to think about and write your answers to the following questions:

- Have I prayed to keep the connection open with the God of my understanding?

- Have I sought through prayer and meditation for freedom from self-will?
- Have I prayed for correct thoughts and actions?
- Have I learned to practice daily meditation?
- Have I prayed, "Your will, not mine, be done"?

Step Twelve: Practice Makes Permanent

Having had a spiritual awakening as the result of these steps, we tried to carry this message to food addicts, and to practice these principles in all our affairs.

Each person's spiritual awakening is unique. The awakening of our spirit as the result of the practice of all of the eleven previous steps sends us out into loving service. There are many ways we can reach out to help others: extend our hand, set up for meetings, make a call to someone who is missing, talk to the newcomer, sponsor others and learn to listen. Where there are no food addiction recovery meetings, our service may be to start one. The Internet has opened a whole new way to carry the message on message boards, in chat rooms and e-mail loops. We talk to the new person, describing our experiences in the disease and in recovery. Because we have "been there," we communicate at an extraordinary level of understanding and strength. We talk the talk—we walk the walk. Our program works! That is our message. How the message is received is not our responsibility. However, whenever anyone, anywhere, reaches out their hand for help, we want help to be there—and for that we are responsible. We support each other, whether long timer or newcomer. We are a family in a very special way—we are members of the fellowship of the spirit. We have learned to live a life based on principles.

What are these principles?

Step One:	Honesty
Step Two:	Hope
Step Three:	Faith
Step Four:	Courage and Self-Knowledge
Step Five:	Integrity
Step Six:	Willingness
Step Seven:	Humility
Step Eight:	Responsibility
Step Nine:	Restitution
Step Ten:	Perseverance
Step Eleven:	Spiritual Growth
Step Twelve:	Love and Service

Our spiritual way of life is practiced in relationship with God and with others. Our Twelve-Step program provides the directions and opportunity to develop the traits of healthy spirituality.

Take some time to think about and write your answers to the following questions:

- Have I conscientiously worked the first eleven steps?
- Do I pass the message on to others both in and out of the fellowship?
- When I fail to practice the principles of a spiritual way of life, do I evaluate and correct my words and actions?
- When I successfully practice the principles of spiritually, do I evaluate and endorse my words and actions?
- What is God doing in my life?

Characteristics of Healthy Spirituality

What does spirituality look like? Galatians 5:22–23 says the fruit of the spirit is love, joy, peace, patience, kindness, goodness, faithfulness, gentleness and self-control. When recovering people talk about being happy, joyous and free, they are describing the traits of their spirituality. It affects everything about us: our relationships, our perceptions and our responses. The development of our spirituality is personal and individual. We will each find our spiritual direction in different ways through prayer, meditation, self-searching, religion, reading, devotions and particularly practicing the Twelve Steps. To me, being spiritual in recovery means living a peaceful, happy, God-filled life in fellowship with others, while becoming free from the attachment to addictive substances and behaviors.

READER/CUSTOMER CARE SURVEY

If you are enjoying this book, please help us serve you better and meet your changing needs by taking a few minutes to complete this survey. Please fold it and drop it in the mail.

As a special **"Thank You"** we'll send you news about new books and a valuable **Gift Certificate!**

PLEASE PRINT   C8C

NAME:_____

ADDRESS: _____

_____

TELEPHONE NUMBER: _____

FAX NUMBER: _____

E-MAIL: _____

WEBSITE: _____

(1) Gender: 1)_____Female 2)_____Male

(2) Age:
1)_____12 or under   5)_____30-39
2)_____13-15   6)_____40-49
3)_____16-19   7)_____50-59
4)_____20-29   8)_____60+

(3) Your Children's Age(s):
Check all that apply.
1)_____6 or Under   3)_____11-14
2)_____7-10   4)_____15-18

(7) Marital Status:
1)_____Married
2)_____Single
3)_____Divorced/Wid.

(8) Was this book
1)_____Purchased for yourself?
2)_____Received as a gift?

(9) How many books do you read a month?
1)_____1   3)_____3
2)_____2   4)_____4+

(10) How did you find out about this book?
Please check ONE.
1)_____Personal Recommendation
2)_____Store Display
3)_____TV/Radio Program
4)_____Bestseller List
5)_____Website
6)_____Advertisement/Article or Book Review
7)_____Catalog or mailing
8)_____Other_____

(11) What FIVE subject areas do you enjoy reading about most?
Rank: 1 (favorite) through 5 (least favorite)
A)_____ Self Development
B)_____ New Age/Alternative Healing
C)_____ Storytelling
D)_____ Spirituality/Inspiration
E)_____ Family and Relationships
F)_____ Health and Nutrition
G)_____ Recovery
H)_____ Business/Professional
I) _____ Entertainment
J) _____ Teen Issues
K)_____ Pets

(16) Where do you purchase most of your books?
Check the top TWO locations.
A)_____ General Bookstore
B)_____ Religious Bookstore
C)_____ Warehouse/Price Club
D)_____ Discount or Other Retail Store
E)_____ Website
F)_____ Book Club/Mail Order

(18) Did you enjoy the stories in this book?
1)_____Almost All
2)_____Few
3)_____Some

(19) What type of magazine do you SUBSCRIBE to?
Check up to FIVE subscription categories.
A)_____ General Inspiration
B)_____ Religious/Devotional
C)_____ Business/Professional
D)_____ World News/Current Events
E)_____ Entertainment
F)_____ Homemaking, Cooking, Crafts
G)_____ Women's Issues
H)_____ Other (please specify) _____

(24) Please indicate your income level
1)_____Student/Retired-fixed income
2)_____Under $25,000
3)_____$25,000-$50,000
4)_____$50,001-$75,000
5)_____$75,001-$100,000
6)_____Over $100,000

FOLD HERE

((25) Do you attend seminars?
1)_____Yes   2)_____No

(26) If you answered yes, what type?
Check all that apply.
   1)_____Business/Financial
   2)_____Motivational
   3)_____Religious/Spiritual
   4)_____Job-related
   5)_____Family/Relationship issues

(31) Are you:
1) A Parent?_____
2) A Grandparent?_____

Thank You!!
The Life Issues Publisher
HCI

Additional comments you would like to make:

_____

_____

_____

_____

N-CS   C8C

8

Abstinence-Based Recovery in the Real World

Our recovery takes place in the real world. We have special needs. It is possible to meet these needs in an unobtrusive way by developing techniques that support recovery. First, we must be willing to do the work of recovery. Secondly, we must be committed to our own recovery. Beyond that, the people that we deal with in the real world will recognize whether we are determined or wishy-washy about getting our needs met. Quiet, courteous determination will be met with cooperation. Sometimes we have to "Just say no!" Say no to ethnic restaurants, say no to offers of addictive foods, say no to dishes topped with addictive substances, say no to people who do not respect our abstinence—including doctors, friends and relatives. We have to demonstrate the strength and courage of our convictions. Addictive substances kill!

There are ways that we can make it easier to meet our recovery needs. The following suggestions are based on my own experience over the years as well as those shared by other recovering food addicts.

Organizing the Kitchen

Remove tempting binge foods from the cupboards and refrigerator. It is best not to have trigger foods readily available. By eliminating junk food from the home, the nutritional value of the family's food will gradually improve. Keep your scales, measuring cups and spoons within easy reach. Have one scale in a small bag for trips to restaurants.

Digital scales are accurate instruments for weighing protein, fruit and potatoes. You may wish to start collecting recipes appropriate for your food plan. Get a food steamer. It is great for steaming grains, protein and vegetables. I use a food processor and blender a lot, too. Find spices and seasonings that are appropriate for the food plan to keep on hand. Those plastic dishes with the airtight tops are great for storage and our "take-outs." Unlike the rest of the country, the recovering food addict's take-out food comes from his or her own kitchen. A cautious reminder: Use glass in the microwave, not those plastic dishes.

Planning

When planning food for the day, it is important to have the food within easy reach. Make it a point to have all of the ingredients in the house for the day's meals in order to avoid making changes and to avoid the added pressure of having to run out to buy ingredients. Check the refrigerator and pantry for needed items as you write your daily plan. An important issue of planning is shopping. Weekly shopping requires a plan, too. In-season produce often guides us in our weekly food selections, because we want the high-quality foods.

Shopping

It is dangerous to shop when you are hungry. Shop after meals. When you are new in recovery, you may wish to take a recovering friend or family member with you to the store if you feel uneasy about shopping alone. Shop with your sponsor the first time around. I take the people I sponsor to the grocery store for a field trip. They have found that very helpful. Keep it simple; have a list and look for products with only one or two ingredients. Stick with whole foods as often as possible.

Look for the freshest, most attractive food; this will make meals special. My first sponsor told me to buy exceptional fruit. Why not? We can have the best of the best. Beware of hidden sugars or starch in products and read the label each time you buy an item. Grains, beans, tofu and other specialty items can be found in a local health food store.

Shop just once a week to limit exposure to the world of addictive substances. One of my sponsees experienced anxiety early in recovery when he went to the grocery store. He was lucky to have a wife to do it for him. Ask for help if it gets rough. It isn't necessary to shop in every aisle of the grocery store. Many of them contain only addictive foods. Avoid those aisles and focus on those items you need for your food plan. It is a good idea to shop with a grocery list in order to avoid impulse buying of trigger foods.

Here is a sample shopping list from the standard grocery store. Check the ingredients list carefully for added sugars, including natural flavors and other indistinguishable ingredients. If you can't identify an ingredient, do not use the product.

Shopping List

baking potatoes
barley
brown rice
cabbage
canned chicken
canned diced
  tomatoes
canned or dried
  beans (black,
  kidney, pinto,
  refried,
  garbanzo)
canned salmon
celery salt
chicken
cinnamon
cooking spray,
  alcohol-free

cottage cheese
dry milk
dry mustard
eggs
fresh fish
fresh fruit
fresh vegetables
frozen vegetables
garlic powder
hamburger, lean
lettuce
milk, nonfat
non-iodized salt
oat bran
oats
oil and vinegar
  dressing
olive or canola oil

onions
pepper
red potatoes
roasted buckwheat
seasoning blends,
  sugar-free
spaghetti and
  pizza sauce,
  sugar-free
squash
sweet potatoes
tofu
tuna, low-sodium
turkey
vinegar
yogurt, plain,
  sugar-free and
  nonfat

You may wish to make a trip to the health food store for products such as the following which may be unavailable in your grocery store.

Adzuki beans
bean sprouts
Braggs Aminos
lentils

millet
organic products
quinoa
rye grain

rye hot cereal
sugar-free chicken
  broth
tempeh

Reporting

After your plan is completed, it is a very helpful practice to report to a sponsor who is experienced in the use of the food plan. In this modern day and age, people phone, e-mail and fax their food plans to their "food sponsor." These sponsors guide the sponsee in the appropriate implementation of the food plan on a daily basis. Once the food has been reported, it is suggested that this report be considered a commitment and that any changes be avoided or discussed with one's sponsor. This allows the sponsee to let go for that day—that is, to be relieved of any further decisions about food for a full twenty-four hours. This relief can help a great deal to reduce obsession with food. Maria found that to be true: "Before I reported my food on a daily basis to a sponsor, I would sit for hours fantasizing about the most delicious meals. Then I came to realize that, although I was physically abstinent, I was still obsessing about food. After I started reporting, the obsession was gone like that!" (She snapped her fingers.)

Accountability is an important principle in recovery. Failing to plan is planning to fail. When we write down our daily food plan and report it to our sponsor, we do not have to worry or obsess about the food for the day. It is a good idea to commit, along with your daily food plan, your program for the day. Report any deviations from your reported food plan. This kind of honest accountability gives us a method of guilt-free eating. Be sure to keep it honest by reporting changes.

Preparation

Many people find it helpful to cook ahead of time and freeze portions that are already weighed and measured. For example, use a rice steamer and prepare several cups of rice. Measure out one-cup servings and put them in plastic bags to store in the freezer. Weigh protein after it is cooked. Grill or bake several chicken breasts, weigh them and freeze for later use. Preparing and freezing complete meals is a time-saver, too. My friends Richard and Penny have a refrigerator that looks like a buffet with abstinent-style barbecue chicken, a large bowl of special coleslaw, fancy baked turkey meatloaf and other great dishes. I use a black iron frying pan for pan and stir-frying. Be sure that cooking spray does not have alcohol as an ingredient.

Zero Trigger Foods

It is our goal to achieve abstinence from all trigger foods. This is the safest way to operate. It is always an unknown how much sugar or other trigger foods our bodies can tolerate before the disease is triggered. We don't know. Therefore the best intention is to achieve absolute abstinence from all trigger substances. One of the major goals of the food plan is to eliminate all foods which will trigger the disease of food addiction at the physical level. Just as an alcoholic absolutely abstains from alcohol in order to recover, food addicts need to identify and abstain from all food substances which will set off active addiction.

Reading Ingredients Lists

Check labels for trigger ingredients. Reading the product list of ingredients is crucial to obtaining and maintaining clean, substance-free recovery. It is impossible to stay abstinent and avoid checking ingredients. The rule of thumb is to check ingredients on every product, every purchase. Processors will change the recipe for their product without fanfare or announcement. (Although there may be a statement that this is the "new and improved product" when sugar in some form is added.) It is our responsibility to stay current on the foods we are eating. One of the canned chicken broth products I commonly purchased added sugar about a year ago. A recent inspection shows that it is gone again. It pays to read those labels! And it is necessary if we wish to remain in clean abstinence. As we go about reading ingredients, it is important to recognize the many names of sugar, flour, wheat and other ingredients which are refined, processed carbohydrates. Best of all, buy fresh and frozen foods that have not been processed and buy whole grains (except wheat).

Restaurant Dining

When ordering in restaurants ask for dry-broiled plain protein, dry baked potato, large vegetable-only salad with no bacon, croutons, eggs, or cheese, with oil and vinegar on the side. Assume the salt is iodized and contains sugar. Beware of sugar added to balsamic vinegar; beware of sugar and starches in marinades, fried foods, all sauces and meat juices (*au jus*). Pass on all of these. Ask the server to hold the bread unless those accompanying you want it.

If the food is not delivered to the table as specified, send it back with clear directions for correcting any errors. Take your cup and scale with you. You might want to carry salt and vinegar. Use camping shakers and bottles that don't leak. If the restaurant does not provide a clean starch such as a baked potato, boiled new potatoes, corn or sweet potatoes, plan ahead to take a starch with you, such as garbanzo beans, to add to a salad.

I do not ask questions in restaurants; servers don't know what is in a dish and it is too time-consuming to ask a server to go to the kitchen to find out. I have also found that talking directly to the chef is not always satisfactory, either. From time to time, if a restaurant is not too busy, I ask to see a container for the list of ingredients. Only if the restaurant is not busy will I ask to speak to the chef about a particular item on the menu. Ninety-nine percent of the time, instead of asking questions, I give very clear directions when ordering, request simple unadorned food and expect my directions to be followed. By giving clear directions, we leave no room for error. In my experience, servers are cooperative and willing to meet our needs.

A client once told me of her experience in a restaurant in early recovery. She asked so many questions and sent food back to the kitchen so many times that all her dinner companions were disgusted. We definitely want to avoid such obnoxious behavior. Keep it simple. Give clear directions, and it will be quite simple to order. Once I was with a group of recovering people. We had to send our orders back several times because the server didn't listen. Another time I had a bad night of it because the chef was creative and thought my fish would be too dry. He added wine! These are the exceptions–the ordering process is usually smooth and effective.

I avoid ethnic restaurants unless an appropriate starch is provided. Sometimes we take brown rice to an Oriental restaurant and eat steamed protein and vegetables. No soy sauce, of course. What if friends or relatives insist on an inappropriate restaurant? Eat before you go, take your food with you or decline the invitation. Our disease loves to have us people-please and go to places where it is impossible to find the kind of food we need.

How Mert Does It

Mert meets the challenge of recovery by taking care of himself. He is a problem-solver with good ideas for us all. This is his story about taking care of his recovery needs when eating in restaurants:

I was told that it would be difficult to eat out all of the time and stay on the food plan. I don't like to cook, although I cook more often now. I don't think there will ever come a time when I will do a lot of cooking, because I am impatient. When I am hungry, I want to eat and I want to get it over with and I don't want to clean up or spend a lot of prep time. What I learned to do was stay abstinent, follow the food plan and eat out. I learned to read labels and get familiar with the names of sugar, as well. I got two digital scales, a large one for the kitchen and a small one I carry in a fanny pack along with a small bottle of salad dressing for my lunch salad. I have a double salad for lunch and two cups of cooked vegetable for dinner.

The thing that was difficult at first was overcoming the thoughts of being embarrassed about taking care of myself. When I go into a restaurant, I make sure to get what I need and pull out my scale. It took me a couple of weeks before I felt comfortable enough to do that. I thought people would look at me. If they do, I just give them a big smile. Today I weigh my baked potato and cut off the excess. I am not a good judge of portion size, so this is not a big price to pay to stay abstinent.

The amazing thing is that in all the restaurants I have visited, the servers will really try to be helpful. I tell them, "I am on a restricted food plan and I need your help." Approaching them in this manner wins their cooperation. Local restaurants which I visit regularly stock brown rice or corn for me. Some restaurants have my lunch ready when I get there. I have gone to conventions and called the meeting planner to find out who is catering the meals; then I call to discuss my restrictions. I have never had one refuse to prepare a meal for me. In one instance, I called ahead and talked to the catering manager, who prepared three special meals for me. At each meal he checked with me personally to see if the meals were all right.

I find it easy to eat out and stay on the food plan. I went to a retreat where most of the food was not on my food plan. At one of the restaurants where I eat, I asked the cook to prepare complete meals from the recovery cookbook. I needed two dinners and two lunches, besides the breakfast meals that I made myself. The restaurant put the meals in containers. There was a refrigerator and microwave available at the retreat. My food was tastier than the food served to the rest of the participants.

Business Lunches

In business situations some of the problems that may arise are the selection of inappropriate restaurants, embarrassment about weighing and measuring, lunches provided by the company and unavailability of appropriate food. When lunches are provided by the company, speak to the caterers to order appropriate meals. If that is not possible, provide your own food. As in every other instance, we cannot rely on others to have the kind of food we will need for our program. In all instances, whether business or social, it is important to plan ahead, call ahead or provide your own food.

Under certain circumstances it might be embarrassing to weigh and measure at business lunches. You may wish to practice using your scale in restaurants before the business lunch. "Eyeballing" food is an inexact way of determining portion size. Some people do it well, others do not. The best practice is to use the scale under all circumstances. If there are times you choose not to weigh and measure, be certain those times are infrequent. Deal with the feelings of embarrassment with your sponsor, therapist or at meetings.

Self-confident individuals who are committed to recovery use their scales regularly.

Travel

Travel requires special arrangements beyond ordering a rental car, arranging a hotel room and buying an airline ticket. When traveling, take all of the food in hand that you will need until you reach your destination and are able to get to a grocery store or restaurant. Don't forget your evening dairy and fruit. On planes, place the food that you will need during the trip on the floor under the seat ahead. Then you will not have to disturb seat mates by getting containers from overhead. I often mix grain, eggs, shredded carrots and spices to make muffins for the trip. I freeze them and carry them in my purse, order a decaf and enjoy. Or I have a salad with protein and starch packed in a disposable container or plastic bag. It has become necessary to carry an extra meal in case a plane is delayed or canceled. It is not always possible to find an suitable meal in an airport.

After arrival at your destination, locate grocery stores, health food stores and restaurants that will fit your needs. In foreign countries find someone who speaks your language in restaurants so that you can communicate your needs. If you cannot find English-speaking servers, plan ahead by having your directions written out in the language of the country. I have had wonderful experiences while traveling and have always found servers who were cooperative and helpful. Sometimes I look for American franchise restaurants where they speak English and have a familiar menu. I store several meals in my room as well as supplemental portions of starch, protein, vegetables and fruit in case I cannot get what I need in a restaurant. I often eat in the hotel dining room or one particular restaurant where they get used to my needs. If there is no refrigerator in your room, ask the restaurant to store your food in their kitchen refrigerator or metabolic and breakfast. If the hotel provides refrigerators in the room, order one. Clear the minibar and use that for your food, too.

Here is a list of things I carry when traveling for a week or more. I use a nylon bag that measures ten by sixteen by nine inches. It is fairly small, and it contains items that will be needed upon arrival. I often put it through with my luggage. Sometimes I carry it on board. It contains:

One small electric cooking pot (Rival)
Canned vegetables, fruit, chicken, tuna, potatoes, beans
Small plastic bags with half-cup portions of raw grain
Plastic bags with one cup frozen brown rice and other
    cooked grains
Spices, decaffeinated instant coffee and tea bags, sweetener
Can opener
Plastic forks, knives, spoons, napkins
A few fresh apples
Raw carrots
Frozen blue ice
A small bowl for eating and mixing and a drinking cup
Measuring cups and spoons
Scale

Upon arrival the bag can be used to store perishable food with ice if a refrigerator is not available. For foreign travel, I take electric converters. I have never been on a package tour where food was provided. I don't think that would work for my recovery. I have been on cruises and ordered all my meals in the dining room as I would in any restaurant. There was no problem staying abstinent there. By planning ahead and making a commitment to abstinence, travel can be a joy.

Relatives and Friends

I was asked recently how to deal with relatives or friends who do not support abstinence. I think it is always important to remember that sometimes these people may be active in addiction themselves. Others are offended by self-discipline because they don't want to live in a disciplined way. Some just do not understand, and still others just want to be in control. It is important to realize that we do not need their support, cooperation, consent, understanding or approval. We find understanding in our meeting rooms from our sponsor, therapist and others in our helping network. We go ahead with our recovery disciplines despite the attitudes of others.

I think it is wise to avoid conversations about recovery with people who are not supportive. It will only lead to needless debate, discussion or argument. Whenever possible, abstain from these people, especially in early recovery during stabilization. Recently a client shared with me that he lost his abstinence in a Thai restaurant because his relatives, whom he was visiting, insisted on eating there. He could have chosen to say, "Where would you like to meet after dinner? I will be eating at six P.M. at the seafood place where I can get the food I need." Or he could have taken his food with him, eaten before going to the restaurant or declined all together. We have options. For recovering people, addictive foods are not an option. People-pleasing is a killer choice.

Going to the Hospital

If your hospital admission is on a nonemergency basis, it is important to make arrangements with the dietitian and physician for the appropriate meal plan. Ask your doctor to write an order to that effect. You may wish to make arrangements with your family or recovering friends and sponsor to bring abstinent meals to you during your hospital stay. That is what Christina did when she was hospitalized. Recovering friends took meals to the hospital until she spoke to the dietitian. The dietitian arranged for a bland diet consisting of "clean" unseasoned foods which were perfect for our plan. Since Christina was very ill, she ate as much of the food as she could, sampling each portion to maintain balance. If your hospital admission is on an emergency basis and you are unable to maintain abstinence during your hospital stay, make arrangements to get abstinent in a safe place before returning to your regular routine. If intravenous fluids are necessary, our doctor friend says, "I believe that normal saline could replace a glucose-rich solution. The key there is to talk with the anesthesiologist before any procedure and ask if intravenous will be necessary. Give him or her information concerning food addiction. Expect doctors to cooperate."

Discuss Orders with Your Doctor

Recently a friend was hospitalized. As a result of her condition, the doctor ordered her to eat two soda crackers "as medicine" to settle her stomach. She followed orders and was triggered by the crackers. She could have discussed an alternative with her doctor. If a starch is necessary, ask if a baked potato will fit the bill. A recovering physician says, "I think the most important thing in the hospital is making sure that hospital personnel know our needs. If we are too vulnerable to take care of ourselves, we need to find a recovering advocate who will assertively, not aggressively, assist in getting our needs met. Doctors don't understand our recovery needs and nurses don't, either. We must protect ourselves."

My dentist told me to use an alcohol-based mouthwash to treat a periodontal condition. I said "no alcohol in my mouth" and explained that I don't use alcohol. He thought for a moment and substituted a 50 percent peroxide solution instead. Take charge of your recovery, take charge of your life.

The Holidays

During the holiday season, it becomes very noticeable in recovery meetings that attendance falls off and our recovering friends start to disappear. Some of these disappearances are long-term and some are permanent. What happens during the holidays? Increased stress is certainly a complicating factor in holiday activities. There is more pressure, date books are fuller, to-do lists become longer, and altogether these are busy times. During these fast-paced times it is tempting to start canceling meetings, forgetting phone calls and postponing step work until after the holidays. After all, isn't this the reason that we recover, in order to enjoy life? The temptation is to take a holiday from recovery.

We have to be vigilant about this kind of complacency and overconfidence. Whatever the excuse for letting up on recovery activities, the "twenty-four-hour principle" of recovery still applies. We must remember that we cannot stay abstinent on yesterday's program. It is crucial to recovery to maintain our program on the twenty-four/seven concept. We work our programs seven days a week, twenty-four hours a day. Each holiday is nothing more than another twenty-four-hour time frame which requires our attention as recovering people. Let us pray that all of us will be guided in recovery through the holidays, making them holy days of joy and peace.

On Holiday from Your Recovery Program?

Before the holidays become frantic, it would be a good idea to outline your "best recovery" program. Formulate a checklist which is based upon those activities which best support recovery. This checklist might include the optimum number of meetings to attend, a commitment to daily phone calls, reading, writing, prayer and meditation. It might look something like this:

Nightly Inventory Checklist

Phoned Sponsor _____

Attended Meeting _____

Exercised _____ hour

Journal Writing _____

Gratitude List _____

Meditation _____ times

Prayer _____

Literature Selection _____

Food Plan

    Planned _____

    Reported _____

    Committed _____

    No Changes _____

Weighed and Measured All Portions _____

Two Phone Calls to _____   _____

Tempting Food and Drink

One of the obvious pitfalls of the holiday season is the abundance of tempting food and drink. All of the magazine covers display in gorgeous splendor all the foods which will trigger our addiction and our life of horror. The whole world has missed the idea that for food addicts those foods should be photographed with a skull-and-crossbones Poison label. For those of us who are food addicted, holiday foods are poison.

Of course, there are always folks who urge us to eat "just a little." People-pleasing is a definite characteristic of many food addicts. When we hear our favorite relative say, "Oooh, I made it just for you. You used to love it," then we have a decision to make. Do we placate our relative or choose recovery? Worse yet, there are others who offer to prepare abstinent food for us, then we show up for dinner to find nothing appropriate for us to eat. Some hostesses even lie about the ingredients, thinking they can "put one over" on us.

The best way to maintain abstinence throughout the holiday orgy of addictive substances is to eliminate or restrict the number of occasions attended, to show up prepared with your own food or to eat before the party. A tactful response to all well-meaning relatives is "No thank you" said with conviction. The bottom line is that I am always responsible for my own recovery and for the food I eat. I have to understand that others don't always understand the importance of physical abstinence. If you trust your host or hostess to understand it, call ahead to make your needs known. Take your scale and measuring cups to facilitate a weighed and measured meal. Don't be your own worst enemy, either. Stop baking those old favorites; the smell alone can trigger cravings. You may wish to stop bringing highly refined and processed foods into your home for the family. Often we stop "pushing those drugs" to our loved ones.

Holiday Compulsive Shopping and Spending

Overspending during the holiday seasons is an issue for many, especially compulsive spenders. The holidays are a good excuse to let loose and really indulge in this addiction. Be aware that much time spent shopping, even without spending large amounts of money, can be an addictive process. Both shopping and spending take us out of reality and away from our daily concerns and responsibilities. We escape into Mall World, where everything is beautiful and all things are possible. We get a false sense of power from the purchase. We become obsessed with it and develop lists of gifts for others, the house and ourselves. The advertisers would have it that we must redecorate the house, purchase a new wardrobe and serve only gourmet food and drink. 'Tis the season to spend, spend, spend. From Halloween to Valentine's Day, we can go on a ninety-day jag.

Credit cards have made it possible to buy now and pay later, mortgaging our future in order to have things now. Huge credit card debt is the burden of many Americans, but it is especially an ordeal for compulsive spenders. Often this spending and debt production is driven by guilt. Addicts often feel "less than" and make an attempt to make it up to loved ones with material goods. Would any of us have the courage to cancel spending next holiday season? I think we would wonder if our loved ones would go on loving us. We are so much the victims of the mass media. Newsprint and television ads relentlessly shout about what we must do and be in order to create a Martha Stewart kind of holiday season.

Take some time to write about the feelings you experience while shopping and spending. Talk about the high of the pursuit, the glitter and glitz of the department stores, the thrill of the music, the spirit of the crowds, the euphoric recall of childhood holidays. Make a list of the ways that you are powerless over spending and shopping. Make a list of the ways that your life has become unmanageable due to that shopping and spending.

In recovery, we must find a way to bring sanity into our world of spending or perish in debt and frustration. There is something joyless about the word "budget!" It is a bucket-of-cold-water kind of word. But we begin to understand that with recovery comes responsibility. In recovery it is finally possible to take charge our financial life. There is power in money management. *How to Turn Your Money Life Around,* by Ruth Hayden, is a wonderful resource for those who are serious about recovery from spending. There are Twelve-Step programs for those who need support in this recovery. If you are interested in more help, you may wish to contact Debtors Anonymous in your area.

The question we may wish to ask ourselves is, "How can I turn my holiday-spending life around without becoming Old Scrooge himself?" The truth is that we can moderate our spending and still celebrate the holidays with love and service instead of guilt and fear. Those are the recovery principles we can emphasize in our lives. By remembering the spirit of each holiday, we may even wish to return to a simpler time of celebration with handmade ornaments or gifts. Let's recount some of the spiritual principles of the holiday season: love, gratitude, kindness, compassion, sharing, caring, joy, humor and play—and let's plan a way to demonstrate those in our lives. Keep the spiritual in mind when shopping; take your Higher Power with you.

Expectations

Too often we have unrealistic expectations of ourselves and others during the holidays. We envision the loving family gathered around the fireplace singing carols and basking in the glow of love. We see ourselves giving and receiving gifts selected with care. The real picture may be somewhat different: dirty dishes, piles of discarded wrapping paper, irritable children and maybe even a cold or flu thrown in for good measure. That's not to say that our holidays are always totally horrible or disagreeable, but they may never match the jolly pictures we conjure up. Projecting outcomes is always dangerous. There is no way to predict the future. Whenever our expectations are high, our serenity is low. Acceptance is the key to serenity.

HALTS

Remember the acronym HALTS, and don't get too Hungry, Angry, Lonely, Tired or Stressed. Avoid overdoing. Stress can trigger food thoughts, so beware of your stress level during the holidays. The tool of HALTS is great for an on-the-spot inventory. If you are experiencing any of these, take immediate action, including relaxation techniques, rest, well-timed meals, meetings and phone calls. Recognition and correction is the key to maintaining recovery.

Feeling Deprived?

Count your blessings, make a gratitude list for after the holidays. Think of how great it will be not to have to go on another diet right after the holidays. One of my dear friends relates how she cried all day on her first holiday in recovery. She felt so deprived. Now she sees that she is deprived of obesity, depression, anger, lethargy, shame, fear, physical pain and medical problems associated with her food addiction. We laugh about having two holiday meals because we stay on schedule and have a turkey dinner midday and one in the evening, too. Those normal eaters usually get just one! We don't have to pass out in front of the TV, either.

Discover Alternatives to Eating and Cooking

There may be something to do over the holidays that does *not* involve baking or eating? What a concept! Get outdoors often to enjoy the winter sun, take a family walk, enjoy a winter sport like skiing or ice skating. It is fun to go to the movies, look at old pictures or home movies and play board games. Of course, here in Florida, we just go on with our usual activities in the sun. Have some fun during the holidays.

The Bottom Line

The bottom line is that for our life-sustaining abstinence, we are responsible. We have to understand that others do not understand. They don't have to understand. We are personally responsible for what we eat and drink, where we eat, how our food is prepared and for provision of that food on a reasonable schedule. No one is allowed to make those choices for us. We must realize that we are worth the time, effort, consideration and cost of recovery—always remembering that the disease costs more.

9

Developing a Program

Recovery Tools

Get a Sponsor!

These are the first words most of us hear when we join a recovery program. A sponsor is a trusted partner in recovery who will share their experience, strength and hope. Sponsorship gives the newcomer a sympathetic, understanding friend when one is needed most. The sponsor provides a connection to other people in the program. Most people are able to find a sponsor at a Twelve-Step meeting. You may wish to have a food plan sponsor and a step sponsor, or the same person may serve as both. One word of caution, though–it can be a serious problem when a sponsee uses two different sponsors to collect differing opinions and plays one against the other.

Sponsors are usually chosen in an informal way. Often, the new person simply approaches a more experienced member who seems compatible and asks that member to be a sponsor. An old saying is "stick with the winners." It is advisable to seek someone who is practicing the program successfully. A good sponsor is experienced in the use of the food plan, practices the steps and has a sponsor who has reached at least one year of back-to-back abstinence. Often in particular areas, no one has long-term abstinence. In that case, there are several options. Some newcomers maintain contact with more experienced people by telephone or e-mail for additional information and support. There is also an emerging phenomenon of co-sponsorship, which entails two individuals sponsoring each other. When a new structured recovery program came to my area, two of us co-sponsored each other with great success. In Canada, where abstinence-based recovery is young, it is common for two people both less than one year abstinent to sponsor each other.

Often a newcomer feels more at ease with a sponsor of similar background and interests. But many recovering people say that they have been most helped by someone who was totally unlike themselves. Keeping the focus on recovery takes focus off the differences. Experience does suggest that it is best for women to sponsor women and men to sponsor men. This is not always possible, due to the shortage of sponsors in strong recovery in some areas. Since there are often smaller numbers of men in recovery, it becomes necessary for women to sponsor men. In this case, it is important to choose stable women with long-term recovery. It is well to understand that a sponsor does not provide such services as a social worker, doctor, banker, taxi driver or counselor. A sponsor is a recovering food addict who helps the newcomer stay abstinent and who shares their experience, strength and hope. It is not professional training that the sponsor offers, but experience in recovery.

Learning to be accountable, we speak to our sponsor on a daily basis to make our food plan and recovery program commitment. Sometimes it becomes necessary to change sponsors. If this is so, we discuss with our sponsor the need to change and the reasons for doing so. We terminate the relationship in a loving way and ask if that person will continue to be available for phone calls.

The day will come when we are asked to be a sponsor. "You can't keep it unless you give it away!" The qualities of a good sponsor are responsibility, honesty, availability, patience and especially good humor. We guard against being hooked into sponsees' resentments. A lesson learned in recovery is to take our own inventories and let others attend to their own. With a sponsor's support, the new person learns that criticizing others is not the recovery way. The job of a good sponsor is to share experience, strength and hope with another.

Recovery Buddies

Find recovery buddies in the program and stick with the winners! Isolation is one of the most dangerous aspects of active addiction. Reach out and break the isolation by developing a support network so you can begin to heal. For older members it is well to remember to avoid returning to isolation. Keep safe people close to you. We have a book of phone numbers that is passed around at our meetings. We list our name, phone number and check one or two columns titled "sponsor" and "buddy." Buddies have gained an official standing in our group and are an important part of our network. It is a good idea to contact people who are newer to the program to give them support and encouragement. We who have suffered from the same addictive disorder speak the same language. Only we can offer help and comfort from the vantage point of the fellow sufferer who has found the way out. We remember the people in our network in our daily prayers and remain available to offer the hand of help to them. For that we are responsible.

Meetings—Out of Isolation

Find a meeting to make your "home group." A home group is where the members watch out for each other, call when one is missing and understand each others' strengths and weaknesses. This is where we find support and fellowship and learn the Twelve Steps. Go to other meetings in your local area, too, because meeting-makers make it! There is a sign in one of our clubs that says, "Many meetings many choices, fewer meetings fewer choices, no meetings no choices."

In order to maintain abstinence from binge food, I think meetings are the single most important factor in recovery. It is there that we give and get the support and information we need to recover. It is there that we are consistently reminded that we have a progressive, chronic, deadly disease. How could we possibly forget that? Believe that we are great "forgetters." I have seen people forget they have a fatal disease and disappear from meetings for years. If you are avoiding going to meetings, take an inventory to identify your resistance or blocks to attending. Work with your sponsor or therapist to overcome these barriers to meeting attendance.

What if there are no abstinence-based meetings in your area? Then it is time to start one. Find one other person who will make a commitment to help you and you are on your way. Find a meeting place, set a time and day and start announcing your meeting. Your meeting will probably be associated with one of the established programs. Contact them for literature and a meeting format.

Attend open AA meetings while you are establishing your own meetings, respecting the request "that all who participate confine their discussion to their problem with alcohol." Open meetings are for anyone interested in the program. It is not opened to food addicts for the discussion of food addiction. Nevertheless, food addicts can learn much about recovery by listening at these meetings. A place to learn about coping effectively is at Twelve-Step meetings. Often the discussion topic at meetings addresses living life on life's terms in order to deal with the stresses of life by acting rather than reacting. Learning, understanding and implementing the principles and practices of the Twelve Steps leads the recovering person into a life that is both spiritually and psychologically sound. There are a number of programs that support recovery from food addiction through various approaches to recovery.

Anonymity—Who, Me?

Anonymity is the practice of true humility. It is the spiritual foundation of our traditions, reminding us to practice the principles embodied in our Twelve Steps. We stop focusing on personalities. This is the end of gossip, backbiting and criticism. We guard against forming bad feelings against other recovering people which might keep us from reaching out to help or be helped. We are all equally valued members of our Twelve-Step groups. Newcomers and old-timers are the same. We have no bosses, just trusted servants. We give God the credit and stay willing to do the footwork.

Telephone—Thirty-Five-Cent Therapy

How about three phone calls a day? Sometimes new people worry that phone calls will be a bother, when actually these calls help both the caller and the receiver. Many food addicts have shared at meetings that they were saved by the bell when a phone call came at just the right time to change a bad moment into a positive one. For the caller, the telephone is a great tool when tempted to deviate from the food plan. Asking for help is the very foundation of recovery. We may hate to do it, but this is a program of ego deflation. When we reach out for help, we are practicing life-saving humility.

Internet Recovery Services—High-Tech Recovery

For those who lack support in their geographical setting, the Internet offers meetings, recovery loops and even sponsorship. The Internet is also an added bonus for those of us who have abstinent meetings to attend. The "net" offers loops, sites and forums where we can find communities sharing information on addiction and recovery from addictive illnesses and eating disorders. This exchange of information contributes to a better understanding of the illness and the process of recovery. We must always be cautious of those who misuse the Internet. As with every other area of recovery, we take the best and leave the rest!

Literature—A Word for the Wise

I heard a speaker once proclaim: Don't binge, do go to meetings, call your sponsor, read the literature and everything will be all right. That is a condensed recovery program in a sentence. Literature serves as our meeting between meetings; from it we learn about the disease of food addiction and recovery. You may wish to read the book *Food Addiction: The Body Knows* in order to learn about the disease process. Each of the Twelve-Step programs offers a selection of conference-approved workbooks, basic texts and pamphlets to guide us in recovery. Take the time to read and learn the message of recovery. Some people find it helpful to read a few pages each day of recovery literature and then share and write on it. Work with your sponsor on which literature is good for you to begin working your program. Starting the day with a recovery thought from one of the daily meditation books has been the practice of many people in good recovery.

Have a Plan

We create a daily plan which states our goals. We become accountable when we report this plan to our sponsor. In the evening, we use it to determine whether we have met our goals. We formulate our plan before reporting to our sponsor for the day. To take an inventory, we must start with a realistic recovery plan made up of activities needed to maintain physical abstinence plus emotional and spiritual growth. A food addict's list might include Twelve-Step recovery meetings, sponsor contacts, food management guidelines, telephone calls, reading recovery literature or listening to recovery tapes, prayer, service and a Twelve-Step study program. Individuals add their own important "musts" to the list in the areas of deportment, spiritual growth, building life skills and therapy. This is our recovery to-do list. Put recovery first. Set realistic goals for the day. You may want to share your list with your sponsor to ensure you are not planning too much. Don't forget to schedule some fun. (See Appendix IV for a sample planner.)

Journaling—The Write Stuff

Many people keep a daily recovery journal. It really helps to write down challenges and insights. You might like to make a Recovery Notebook. Use a three-ring binder and reserve sections for journaling and daily planning, which includes food plan, inventory, step work, gratitude list and exercise record. You may be thinking, *But I don't like to write. I don't know how or what to write. It seems like being back in school.* One way to get started is to just let it rip. Write free-flowing text, don't even bother to punctuate or capitalize. Just let the thoughts pour out. Keep it short if you want. This isn't an assignment that is going to be red-penciled by your teacher. It is an outpouring of your own thoughts and ideas *just for you.* The wonderful thing about journaling is that in later years you can go back and review your growth and change.

Use your journal to deal with pain. Pain is like a knock on the door. It is a signal that something needs attention. We can respond by running and hiding, unwilling to face the messenger. We can respond with anger by fighting against the messenger. Or we can listen to the message to see where that takes us. Journal writing will help us face the feeling and find the message; from that comes growth and change.

Make a gratitude list part of your journal experience, listing five to ten items each day. Maintaining an attitude of gratitude keeps us positive. As addicts, it is so easy to slip into self-pity and negativity. Our gratitude list puts things in perspective as we focus on our gifts and miracles.

Recovery Practices—A Way of Life

Service

In *Dr. Bob and the Good Oldtimers*, Dr. Bob Smith, one of the co-founders of Alcoholics Anonymous, relates that he had been a member of the Oxford Group for two and a half years and Bill Wilson, the other co-founder, had been a member for five months. Bill had managed to stay sober while Bob continued to drink. There was a significant difference between the two. Dr. Bob says, "Bill had acquired their idea of service. I had not." The book goes on to say, "This idea, which Bill brought and Dr. Bob never forgot was put into action immediately. They started trying to help yet another drunk."

The concept of service is pretty clear. It is the culmination of all of our steps of recovery, the last words of which are these: ". . . we tried to carry this message to food addicts and to practice these principles in all our affairs." Our recovery depends on service. In our first day, week or month of recovery we can find a way to offer service by opening and setting up for meetings, making phone calls and showing up for meetings. When we have been around for awhile, we will become involved in other levels of service on the group level by leading meetings, serving as group secretary, then moving onto other levels of service such as intergroup or world service representative. Survival of the fellowship and survival of the individual is dependent on these kinds of service. We have to "suit up" and "show up" in order to survive.

Prayer and Meditation

When practiced regularly, prayer and meditation can change the way we deal with life in a very fundamental way. Who among us has not used the Serenity Prayer in times of stress? It could be called the Release from Stress Prayer.

> *God grant me the serenity*
> *To accept the things I cannot change,*
> *Courage to change the things I can,*
> *And wisdom to know the difference.*

The gift of this prayer is that it applies simple logic to difficulties.

Can I change it? Yes. Then change it!
Can I change it? No. Then accept it!

Eventually, we recognize we can change only what we see, what we think, what we say and what we do. The rest is beyond our control. When God grants us the wisdom and courage to change ourselves and leave the rest to him, we find serenity.

Here is my recovery prayer: "God, you have given me awareness, strength and power to challenge the thoughts that take me off my path of peace. Today I choose to cooperate with your will and accept your grace. With your help, I turn away from inappropriate thoughts of food. I turn away from thoughts of criticism and blame of myself and others. Lead me on the path of love and service."

Meditation is a quiet time for being in the moment, learning about sitting quietly in the present. We stop chatter, planning, scheming and rushing about and put aside some time for peace. Training in various forms of meditation is available. Check the phone book for opportunities in your area. Or you may wish to use a guided meditation tape for your quiet time. Check your library or the Internet for ideas and opportunities to learn about meditation.

Forgiveness

Upon first thought it seems that we are meant to forgive others who have done something wrong. However, in order to come to that conclusion, we have to judge that person in terms of right and wrong, otherwise forgiveness would be unnecessary. Maybe we need to look at our judgments as the basis of the problem. When we judge others we become angry, when we judge ourselves we feel guilty. Spiritually, anger and guilt have no value, they are toxic emotions. The way out of the pain of anger and guilt is to suspend judgment. When we give up the judgment, we give up the pain of anger and guilt.

How can we do this? First, by examining the judgment. In order to create pain, we create subjective judgments dealing in right and wrong, good and bad, coulds and shoulds. In the world of the spirit there is no right/wrong, good/bad, could/should–just love and acceptance. Our spiritual path is learning to love and accept. The other choice is to live in the pain of unforgiveness, resentment, anxiety and guilt. Judgment and resentment of others is like drinking poison and hoping the other person will die. Resentment spoils our lives and the lives of those around us. When we give up judging, we no longer create resentment and guilt. We learn to love and accept others just the way they are today. Bless them, change me.

How can we take our own inventory without creating guilty feelings? We drop the judgment. If we were perfect, we wouldn't need God or each other. Instead, we recognize that we are each a work in progress. By recognition and correction of our failures, we grow spiritually. Daily, we evaluate our conduct against our own rules established with the help of the people in our support network. With the help of our sponsor, we develop a checklist determining what constitutes our most effective recovery program and course of conduct. We may wish to consult our therapists and clerics for feedback as well. We then use the checklist for our evening inventory. When we fall short of our goals, we evaluate and correct our attitudes and actions. When we meet our goals, we endorse ourselves for making progress in recovery.

Acceptance

Acceptance is a principle discussed in recovery meetings. Imagine for a moment what the practice of absolute acceptance could do for us! If we could practice acceptance at its highest level, no problem could exist for us. In the state of pure acceptance there could be no expectations, criticism, blame, judgment, anger, hostility, fear, self-righteousness, condemnation or any other negative state we could describe— only peace. On a more practical note, however, since no one reaches perfection, the degree of acceptance we are able to practice results in a corresponding degree of peace. As explained in the book of *Alcoholics Anonymous,* when you judge people and situations as unacceptable, you become agitated and disturbed. However, when you learn to change yourself and your response to situations, you find peace.

A Daily Inventory

Life is a cinch by the inch and hard by the yard! That is why it is a good idea to evaluate our recovery process daily, before life swings out of control. When we see that our decisions, behaviors, attitudes and motives are effective, we evaluate and endorse them. When we see that they are ineffective, we evaluate and correct them. With the help of the members in our support network, we can develop interventions to deal with our ineffective choices. Sadly, some food addicts report they use their inventory to beat themselves up. Such an inclination is counterproductive to recovery. In taking inventory, we avoid guilt promotion by realizing our inventory is about growth and change. It is not about being "good" or "bad." We strive to remember the course of our recovery is one of progress, not perfection. We can neither know we are making progress, nor can we halt the destructive process, unless we are honestly aware of our daily choices. An evening review of our daily activities aids in the identification of actions that either add or detract from the growth process. This daily evaluation keeps us from developing destructive patterns that will undermine our recovery process.

Conscious Eating

You might enjoy practicing a more peaceful way of eating. This experience is best suited for a quiet time when the kids are at school and the telephone is turned off. Play some soft music. Plan to be silent. Abstain from drinking, because food addicts often use drink to flush food down. Prepare your food so that there will be no interruptions during the meditation. If you need salt, pepper or other condiments, get them before starting.

Take a moment to relax and get centered. Make a conscious commitment to this meal by saying, "I consciously choose this meal. It is just the right amount." Notice whether you are experiencing any emotions at this time. Begin to eat, take a mouthful of food, put down your utensil, chew and swallow. When you finish your first bite, take another, put down your utensil, chew and swallow. Take time to taste your food. Proceed, eating in this manner at your own pace.

Notice if you find it difficult to wait. Are you used to working your plate? That means maintaining contact with your food by stirring it around with your fork. Notice if you want to play with your food while chewing. These exercises were developed to raise awareness of your eating patterns. While doing them, you are changing your relationship with food. You are learning to make conscious adult decisions about how you eat and what you eat. As you slow down your eating behavior, you have a chance to experience the taste and texture of your food. You are retraining your hand to break contact with the food and to slow down the process of eating. Be sure to taste your food to satisfy mouth hunger. Get in touch with your feelings–are you frustrated, grateful, resentful, worried or enjoying this meal? Get in touch with all of the thoughts you are having about it. These are areas of consciousness that you might like to develop around eating. You may wish to tape-record these instructions, along with background music and a thought for the day, so that you can repeat the experience at another time.

Hydrating the Body—Water, Water Everywhere

Water is part of the food plan. The body needs water. Sometimes we have to remind ourselves of the obvious. We may find ourselves wandering around looking for something good to drink, probably because we are so turned on to good tastes. By eliminating all of the presweetened products, we are left with water to drink. Recovery is a wonderful thing, because that is exactly what the body needs. Most folks are not getting enough water. Dehydration leads to fatigue, lowered endurance and performance, as well as feelings of hunger.

It is a good idea to follow conventional wisdom by drinking at least eight, eight-ounce servings of water per day. Men may even need more, probably nine to twelve servings per day. The more time spent outside, the more water is needed to replenish lost fluids. It is not a good idea to wait until we are thirsty to drink water. By that time, we probably have already lost two or more cups of total body water. It is a good idea to drink during the day, so having a bottle in the car, in the office and around the house prompts regular water consumption. We are fortunate to be off caffeine and alcohol because they dehydrate the body. When exercising, we want to keep on drinking. It is a good idea to carry a bottle of water during exercise. Regular sipping seems to be the most efficient means of hydration. Also, because there is water loss during sleep, start and end the day with a glass of water. When ill with colds or flu, which tend to dehydrate, be sure to keep on drinking that water.

Massage

Our goal is to achieve good health and balance. Massage and other forms of body work are excellent choices to reduce stress, fatigue and chronic pain. Massage enhances recovery from years of food abuse by restoring metabolic balance. It offers many healing benefits, including improved circulation. Oxygen and nutrient supplies to muscles, joints, organs and the brain are increased. There is a calming effect to the nerves and improved elimination of metabolic wastes. For this reason, your massage therapist will probably remind you to drink plenty of water after the procedure. Massage is effective in reducing the pain of spasm, inflammation and tissue damage. For food addicts with body-image issues, massage is a positive step forward in recovery. Choose your massage therapist carefully and discuss sensitive issues with him or her.

Good Nutrition and Vitamins

A well-nourished body does not call out for more food. Good nutrition supports recovery in a realistic way. Implementing the food plan provides a major shift from a very low level of nutrition to a much improved one. It's important to eat enough protein, vegetables and complex carbohydrates to supply our bodies with needed nutrients to keep our metabolism functioning efficiently. Emphasis on high-quality food choices such as whole grains, soy products, lean meat, low-fat dairy products, fresh fruit and vegetables will improve the caliber of our nutrition. A high percentage of the population doesn't get the amounts of vitamins and minerals needed, resulting in deficiencies of these nutrients. Vitamins and minerals keep metabolism operating at peak efficiency. Optimize your intake by supplementing with a daily vitamin-mineral product. (Remember to check labels carefully as some vitamins contain wheat fillers.) Start with a good multivitamin and mineral complex, which will provide you with a foundation of antioxidants, B vitamins and essential minerals. You might wish to add extra nutrients for your body's special needs.

When working with a nutritionist, locate one who respects the concept of abstinence-based recovery.

Rest and Relaxation

Busy schedules often leave us with limited time for rest and relaxation. Our bodies require adequate time to slow down in order to restore themselves. Healthy choices support good recovery. The years spent in addiction take their toll. Recovery requires rest and relaxation. Our bodies have been stressed by addiction, withdrawal and other challenges of early recovery. During these times of extreme stress, we need more rest than we will require later in recovery. This is because our bodies use the rest cycle to repair the damage of years of abuse. Daily activity levels determine the amount of sleep the body requires.

Achieving adequate sleep depends on the discipline of establishing a regular bedtime routine for retiring and rising. Sleep problems? Napping may interfere with nighttime sleep, so you may want to eliminate it. Avoid decaf coffee if you have sleep difficulties. Even decaf contains some caffeine. Because of genetic predisposition to addiction, we would always avoid the use of sleeping pills. Don't leave out the fruit and dairy before bed. It provides just the right amount of carbohydrate to feed the sleeping brain for eight hours.

Some food addicts suffer from sleep apnea, a disorder characterized by loud snoring interrupted by stopped breathing, followed by a gasp as breathing resumes. Consult a doctor if you have those symptoms. Sleep apnea is usually resolved after weight loss. If you have "binge" dreams—waking up to the belief that you had a food binge—be assured that this is a fairly common phenomenon in early recovery. It is the mind's way of cleaning out old ideas. After a moment of panic, we feel tremendous relief that we didn't binge at all.

To promote good sleep, think good thoughts, establish a relaxing nighttime routine, avoid stimulation such as television, work or worry before bed. Happy dreams!

Exercise

Moderate exercise meets our recovery goal of bringing the spirit, mind and body into balance. If you are just beginning, start out slowly. Avoid exercising to the point of pain. Be sure to get your doctor's okay for your exercise plan. When you are conditioned, plan to spend thirty to forty-five minutes at least three times a week doing aerobic exercise, such as aerobics training, running, walking, biking or swimming, with stretching for flexibility before and after. Weight training on alternate days will provide a good exercise program. Look for opportunities for exercise programs in your area. Exercising outdoors in the fresh air and sunshine is an added dimension. Sunlight is a mood-enhancer. We need at least fifteen minutes of sunshine each day for healthy function of the pineal gland and our endocrine system. Avoid seasonal affective disorder (SAD) by getting a daily dose of sunshine.

Humor and Play—The Safe Way to Alter Mood

Life is a serious matter! But some folks tend to take themselves too seriously. Lots of us have developed inhibitions to play and laughter. There is a growing body of research and literature on how humor and play contribute to health and well-being. In his book, *Head First: The Biology of Hope and the Healing Power of the Human Spirit,* Norman Cousins enlightened us on how humor can positively affect health. This is the most delightful way to bring our brain and body chemistry into healthy balance! On one occasion when I was presenting a humor and play workshop, I realized how great I felt while organizing it. I had been giggling for a week. Here is a challenge: just try to be sad while skipping around a big room, or paste a big grin on your face and go ahead and try to get depressed. Laughter is good for us. It is good for our bodies and minds. We always feel great after a meeting where there are lots of laughs. Part of growing up in recovery is learning to laugh at ourselves. Healing humor is the type that unites us. That's why things are so funny in recovery meetings where we focus on our common idiosyncrasies. We've all been there and done that! So why not take five minutes to do something playful, silly and fun?

Healing Body Image

Body image is really a self-esteem issue, which takes a terrific beating while we are in the disease of food addiction. We try so many things to deal with the disease, and we are doomed to failure until we get the right information and the right support. We begin to see ourselves as failures. We blame and berate ourselves. It takes time in recovery to begin to see that we were not at fault; we have an addictive illness. It all takes time.

The greatest gift we can give ourselves is time to grow in self-acceptance and love. No matter which way our disease manifests itself outwardly, the results are the same for all of us: No amount of food or other substance will fill that void inside. No amount of starving or purging will rid us of self-hate. God made us in his image. He gave us free will to choose the path we want to follow. He made each of us differently—different shapes, different sizes, different intellects, different wants and needs. He gives each of us different gifts and talents, with the power to develop those gifts and talents through his love and grace.

Our bodies are God's temple here on Earth. We cannot get closer to God until we are willing to treat our bodies with the acceptance, love and gentleness that he intended. Our security, our sense of self-worth and our usefulness to God and to our fellows comes not from how we look to the world, but from where we are in relation to God.

My Body Affirmation

My body is a good place to live. I am glad that I have chosen this particular body because it is right for me. It is the right size and shape and color. It serves me well. My body is a miracle. I choose the healing thoughts that create and maintain my healthy body and make me feel good. I love and appreciate my body just the way it is today. I choose to focus on what is right with my body today.

Affirmations

Affirmations are carefully constructed statements designed to challenge self-defeating thoughts and beliefs and change them into self-enhancing ones. They are positive, personal and written in the present tense. We could change the Serenity Prayer from a prayer of supplication to an affirmation with the change of one letter. Here goes: God, grant me the serenity to accept the things I cannot change, courage to change the things I can and wisdom to know the difference. In this prayer we are asking for something. Here is the affirmation: God *grants* me the serenity to accept the things I cannot change, courage to change the things I can and wisdom to know the difference. Now we have affirmed something. It is an altogether different idea.

Once we develop an affirmation that best suits our situation, we can write it, say it out loud, as well as tape and listen to it. When the affirmation becomes believable we will start to see positive results in our lives—our self-defeating belief has been changed.

Music

Feeling savage or beastly? Soothe yourself by turning on some music and listening to its healing vibrations. Music creates a response both physical and psychological.

The sound of music has been used for centuries to alter mood: drumming, chanting, song and dance are healthy outlets. It has been used for its invigorating, calming or spiritual effects. Lanie, a music teacher, says, "God thought so highly of music that he dedicated one of his sixty-six books to music: Psalms." A wise young man named Paul, who has never used drugs or alcohol, says he turns on calming classical music when feeling anxious or frustrated. A friend relates that when she was a child, she played selections on the piano when she was angry. As she played, the feelings vanished. Select music to create the desired response and spend some time to let your body, mind and spirit respond.

10

Dealing with Feelings

During our development, we formed certain beliefs. Many of these come from childhood. Each of our beliefs, whether rational or irrational, generates ideas and thoughts. We react or respond to such thoughts. Rational thoughts produce favorable feelings, and irrational thoughts produce toxic feelings. Because we have used food for so many years instead of growing and maturing, we continue to act out our old childhood beliefs. Addiction keeps us stuck mentally and emotionally in childhood. Those old childish beliefs affect our thinking. Irrational beliefs produce irrational ideas. Those ideas in turn produce painful, toxic feelings. Actually, we cannot have a pain without a thought. We are victimized by the thoughts we think and the feelings produced, not the people we blame.

We who are addicted tend to react to toxic feelings in an addictive way. We "eat over" them. We eat to numb or soothe those feelings. Now we reach for our recovery tools instead of into the refrigerator. There are no solutions in there! When we stop using food to numb our toxic feelings, we must find ways to deal with them. Without our drug, strong feelings surface. Instead of reaching for food to dull the pain, we learn to face our feelings. They are the messengers that signal there is work to be done. We may believe that we are victims of our feelings, but actually we create them. Since we produce our thoughts, we produce our emotions, too. The key is that feelings follow thoughts. If we are willing to change the thought, a new feeling will follow. Unchecked, the addictive pattern looks like this:

Diagram One

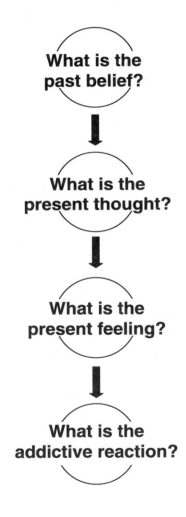

For example, one day I was walking my little miniature schnauzer. As we passed my neighbor's house, their muscular pit bull escaped the house and charged my little dog. There was a vicious dog fight at the end of the leash. I pulled on it, got my dog out of there, picked her up and ran for home. Fortunately, neither of us was injured physically. Psychologically, my injury had just begun.

After that occurrence, I seemed to be noticing a lot of loose dogs and felt scared of them. Even one tall dog behind a low fence frightened me. Another vicious barker on the end of a chain was terrifying, too. This was new. I had never been afraid of dogs before. In fact, I had been the one who caught the neighborhood strays and took them home.

Another incident occurred one day as I was walking my dog. When we reached the corner there was a very large dog standing on the sidewalk. At that point, my fear was negatively affecting my personality, because I called out to the owner, "We have leash laws, that dog should be on a leash." He didn't respond. The dog started walking toward us and I started screaming. The man said, "Lady, you are a maniac!" I was hysterically afraid of that dog. On some level, I knew that was a big old safe dog, but my powerful belief was creating enormous fear. Since I was in recovery and didn't choose to act addictively over my anxiety, I went home and went to work on my fears. This had gone on long enough!

Here is the model that I use to work on feelings:

1. Identify the feeling.
2. Identify the thought.

3. Challenge the thought.
4. Change the thought.

The first step is to identify the feeling. Second, write down the thought that produced it. If possible, identify the belief that created the feeling. Then write down the immediate reaction. Then go back to the top circle and identify the old belief.

Present Feeling: Fear
Present Thought: This dog is dangerous.
Past Belief: Loose dogs are dangerous.
Reaction: Scream

The next step was to challenge the thought:

Is that thought kind?
Is that thought helpful?
Is that thought true?

The thought was not true, kind or helpful. I answered no to all of them. My problem was not the dog on the sidewalk, my problem was my perception of that dog. I was the problem! Just think of how may people walked by that dog without screaming. I suppose everyone did. I needed to change my thought. What was a secure thought that would change my thoughts and reactions to loose dogs? "I am safe and secure as I walk in my neighborhood." After that, the problem went away. Here it is many years later and I no longer meet loose dogs on my walks around the neighborhood. Unresolved life situations will continually come up for resolution. Those that are resolved, disappear. That seems simplistic, but it is true for me.

In the manner described, we can change our emotional health. It is a simple as changing our perceptions and self-talk. On the other hand, it requires conscious effort, application and practice. The more we practice challenging and changing our irrational ideas, the more emotionally stable we will become. As part of our Tenth Step evening review, we work on toxic feelings. Feelings are the messengers that call for our attention. When they are ignored, there is always something we can use to block the pain: shopping, spending, computers, television and other substances. Rather than do something addictive to anesthetize the pain, we quickly review our day for strong feelings. Resolve the feeling by going through this kind of process.

Self-defeating beliefs and ideas will continue to plague us until they are challenged. The glorious outcome of this kind of work is this: We do our work on the present thought and feeling. Because of this, we heal the future by eliminating addictive reactions. We heal the past as well, because we challenge and change past beliefs. We learn that misery is a choice and that better choices are available. We make an active effort by ourselves or with the help of our sponsor to choose a better way. In recovery, we are able to examine our beliefs and thoughts in order to grow. Here is a diagram of the recovery process at work:

Diagram Two

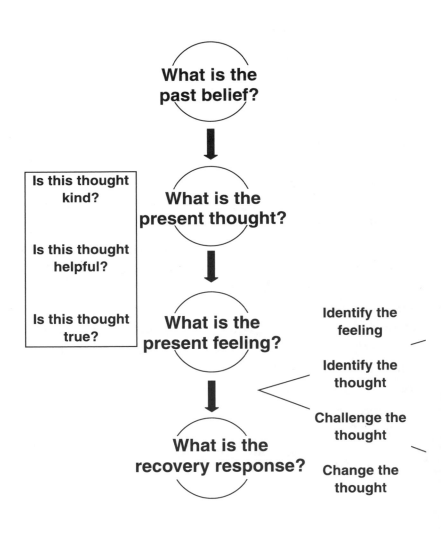

In recovery, the response would be to check the feeling during the evening Tenth Step inventory by doing the work in a way such as in the questionnaire that follows.

A Worksheet Questionnaire

Identify a strong feeling you experienced today._____

_____ (Be sure to use feeling words: anger, sadness, fear.)

Express the thought that preceded the feeling. _____

What was your automatic reaction (usually something addictive)?_____

Describe your belief (message from the past) that is the foundation for your thought. _____

Challenge the thought:

Is that thought kind? _____

Is that thought helpful? _____

Is that thought true? _____

Beware of this one. Because it comes from our belief system, it seems true. However, if it is not kind or helpful, it cannot be true. If it is true, it cannot produce toxic emotions. Reminder: If the thought is not kind, true or helpful, it is irrational. Irrational thoughts produce toxic feelings.

Change the thought to one that is kind, true and helpful.

_____

_____

_____

_____

Kind, true and helpful thoughts produce peaceful, nontoxic
feelings. When I am in conflict with another person I
change the thought to this: "I love and accept _____

_____

_____

just the way he or she is today, because love and acceptance
are spiritual principles and I choose to live a spiritual way of
life."

How do you feel now? _____

_____

_____

_____

11

Overcoming the Barriers to Recovery

Barriers to recovery are situations, beliefs and behaviors which serve to block good recovery and place it in peril. These obstacles keep us from developing a good program from the outset. They include characteristics and attitudes developed during the disease process which must be overcome in order to grow in recovery. It is important to use all of our recovery tools to identify and eliminate these barriers.

Lacks Good Information

Good information supports recovery in two important areas. First, it is important to recognize that food addiction is a physical phenomenon with recognizable progression, triggered by specific substances. Secondly, we need a food plan that works by eliminating those triggers. Without this information, we run the risk of remaining in the disease while struggling to find a way out. Many individuals attend Twelve-Step meetings for years and never arrive at a workable definition of abstinence. One of the greatest struggles in recovery is defining abstinence in order to obtain and maintain physical recovery. Some who have difficulty staying abstinent never get physically clean and therefore are always triggered. When a food addict ingests even a small amount of addictive foods, cravings and the urge to binge are triggered. In order to get clean and live free of cravings and urges, the food addict needs to be aware of every ingredient that is eaten. This kind of enlightened eating results in relief from craving. Zero addictive food triggers is the goal of the well-informed.

Never Completes Detox

One of the greatest struggles in recovery is achieving clean abstinence in order to obtain and maintain physical stabilization. Some who have difficulty staying abstinent never get physically detoxed. When a food addict eats even a small amount of addictive substances, cravings will be triggered along with the urge to binge. In order to get clean and stay that way, a food addicts needs to read labels, know the names of addictive ingredients, eat only clean foods, order assertively in restaurants, shun so-called sugar-free presweetened products, avoid mixtures prepared by others, learn to eat simply, be prepared by planning ahead, accept responsibility for all food choices and leave nothing to chance. Informed eating results in relief from craving.

Minimizes Food Addiction

A crowd of recovering food addicts had dinner recently with a morbidly obese gentleman who stated, "I know I could die from drinking too much, but no one ever died from eating too much!" Often food addiction is seen as a little problem, certainly nothing like alcoholism or heroin addiction. Let's look at the consequences of this "little problem." A life of poor health–physically, mentally, emotionally and spiritually–and early death are not to be treated lightly. The result of staying in the disease process is a high price to pay for minimizing addiction. Food addiction may be perceived as merely a weight problem and not an addiction at all. Focusing on weight as the problem and weight loss as the solution will keep a food addict in a vicious cycle of weight losses and gains, during which the disease remains active, with deadly results. This is a chronic, progressive and fatal disease. To understand the impact of food addiction, it is a good idea to list our personal consequences, including the effect on family, friends, physical health, career, mental health, values and attitudes. Identifying these painful consequences changes our perception of the illness.

Believing the Lies the Disease Tells

Sometimes it is helpful to see the disease as a separate entity. By separating from it, we can objectively view its influence on us. What are some of the lies it whispers in our ear?

"Why not have just one and go back on your food plan tomorrow?"

Just "one" will trigger the disease and put me back in hell!

"Surely it would be all right to have a little cake on your birthday."

A little cake is all it would take to ruin my birthday with guilt and my life with disease.

"You can do it alone, you don't need a program."

Isolation is the breeding place of addiction.

"Nobody will know if you eat that."
My body will always recognize addictive substances and trigger the addictive process.
"One bite won't hurt."
One bite is too many and a thousand not enough.
"You will feel better after you eat."
We eat, to feel better, those foods that make us feel worse.
"You can handle it."
This is a progressive disease. The consequences of eating addictive foods will be worse this time.
"You are not a 'real' food addict."
I admitted that I was powerless over food and that my life had become unmanageable.
"You need me; you can't live without me."
Wrong! With you I die.
"This time it will be different."
Yes, it will be different–it will be worse.
"You are not hurting anyone but yourself."
Then why do I have so many amends to make?
"You can start tomorrow."
Tomorrow never comes. Abstinence now!
"It will be different this time, you have control."
I am powerless. Trying to control trigger foods is like trying to control diarrhea.
"The food will kill the pain."
That food will create more pain than I can imagine.
"It won't kill you this time."
It will kill everything good in my life: physical, mental and spiritual progress.
"It will make everything better."

The pain will be unbearable.

"A little bite of food can't possibly have more power than you."

It has the power to drive me to the brink of suicide and death.

A dear friend called this morning. She has been trying to eat herself to death for the past week. She has been in and out of hospitals and psychiatric wards. The disease told her it was safe to eat a dangerous corn product after eight years of good recovery. She has been suffering for the past five years. We have a disease that tells us we don't have a disease. It tells us many other lies too: that we are not really powerless because we can handle binge food and go right back on our plans. If any of this were so, we would not need a plan or a program. In fact, if this were so, we would have stopped reading this book long ago. Every lie that the disease tells must be countered with a rational recovery thought. Each false thought blocks the memory of the pain of the addiction. When the pain is recalled to counter the lies, we can get back on track again. Believing the lies puts us back into the full-blown disease with all its horrible consequences. A First-Step review of all the consequences of the disease will counteract the seductive lies the disease tells us.

Perfectionism—Frequently Linked with Eating Disorders

Work for a grade of B. If you gasped at the very thought of anything less than a grade of A, keep on reading.

Perfectionism is paralyzing. "If I can't do it perfectly, I won't do it at all." Many relapses spring from such an idea. One small mistake in the food plan results in the decision to ditch the whole thing. Perfectionists don't recognize that "Perfect is impossible!" Some of the characteristics of perfectionism are:

- High expectations of self and others
- Unrealistic standards
- Extreme personal pressure to perform
- Rigidity
- Self-worth based upon performance
- Procrastination due to fear of failure
- High stress, anxiety and fatigue from worry
- Guilt when performance falls short
- Lack of enjoyment from accomplishments
- Intolerance of others' shortcomings
- Compulsive overdoing

The remedy requires recognition, admission, acceptance and action. Recognition is the first step. One friend has her family help her spot perfectionistic characteristics. They treat it with humor, calling out "You just did the P-thing again!" The next step is to admit when perfectionistic attitudes create pain for oneself and others and to accept that we are fallible human beings who make mistakes and experience setbacks. A way to manage perfectionism is to identify the associated feelings, which may be anxiety, frustration and fear of failure. The next step is to identify the thought that generated the feeling: "My house must be perfectly clean and neat for company." Challenge the thought:

Is it kind, true and helpful? If not, change the thought. "Our guests will enjoy a relaxed, happy atmosphere. My house-keeping is good enough." Georgeanne leaves a wrinkle in her bedspread to counteract her tendency to want the room to look perfect. Mary reminds herself that she is a human being, not a human doing, and that it is okay to relax and just "be." Find creative ways to counteract a tendency toward perfectionism.

Wants It "My Way"

A friend in recovery shared with me the story of her first weeks in program. She told her sponsor that she wanted to change the food plan to suit herself—less of this, more of that. Her sponsor asked, "How much do you weigh?" My friend responded with her current weight, which was her lifetime high. Her sponsor said, "That's where your best thinking got you!" The AA book says, "Some of us have tried to hold on to our old ideas and the result was nil until we let go absolutely." It is certainly dangerous to apply all of those old diet ideas to the food plan. One of the basic elements of recovery is to learn to follow directions. "My way," our ego, keeps us in the illness.

Minimal Commitment

The person who is minimally committed to recovery lacks the resolve, willingness to sacrifice, discipline and spirit of obedience that are required. The AA book tells us, "Half measures availed us nothing." This sounds like a tough order, but let's face it–recovery is a task for the desperate. We look for an easier, softer way but cannot find one. Anne says, "Every plan I have tried was unsuited for the treatment of my disease. Nothing worked until I found the formula– the Recovery Food Plan." After trying every other avenue to no avail, we become ready to do the work of recovery. The consequences of staying in the disease become far too painful. Learning a new way of living pays off in health, happiness, joy and freedom.

Self-Reliance

On the face of it, self-reliance seems like a good thing, but when it comes to recovery from addiction it is different: We ask for help or perish! In recovery, we come to believe that alone we are powerless over food. After all, haven't we tried everything we can think of on our own? From AA literature, we learned that we came into recovery "expecting to be taught self-confidence. Then we had been told that . . . self-confidence was no good whatever; in fact, it was a total liability. There was no such thing as personal conquest of the . . . compulsion by the unaided will" (*Twelve Steps and Twelve Traditions*). We come to rely upon the program, the God of our understanding, our sponsor and those people who make up our support network. That which sounds so horrifying to the self-reliant soul becomes our great gift and blessing. As we reach out to give and receive help, we learn that what we really give and receive is love. Love replaces self-reliance, and we become part of a greater whole. The love of one food addict for another has no equivalent in the world of the disease, because it is love without a price tag.

Negotiating with the Food Plan

Each element of the food plan was designed to address the various aspects of the disease. Because of this, each principle of the food plan is important to the success of our recovery. Changes create unnecessary complications. The disease will always take advantage of every compromise we make with abstinence. The major role of the food plan is to eliminate addictive substances. Adding foods that seem all right, because they are not sugar, flour or wheat, is an unfortunate route frequently taken. It is the road to disaster. Reducing the amount of protein in the food plan or eating carbohydrates without a protein will trigger cravings. Maintaining balance between protein and carbohydrates is favorable to our brain chemistry and thus our recovery, because the amino acids in the protein foods moderate the production of brain serotonin. Weighing and measuring is the way we manage volume, yet we may arrive at restaurants without scales. This puts us in a "slippery place" without a way to manage volume. Careful scheduling is essential to keep metabolism level. Level metabolism leads to physical and emotional stability. Sometimes we hear from food addicts who waited too long for a meal and experienced the pain and emotional liability of low blood glucose or, worse yet, missed a meal. Missing meals is the fast track to relapse.

Believes Food Processors

"I believed in those no-sugar-added products. Now I read every label. Those food processors are such liars!" says one recovering food addict, who saw the light and began to realize that sugar-free usually means sugar-full. She was on the food plan as written until she added one of those so-called "sugar-free" foods. That decision led her to an all-time high weight of two hundred eighty-nine pounds. When food processors write sugar-free across the label, be suspicious and check the list of ingredients very carefully. If you identify an ingredient of which you are unsure, do not use the product.

After reviewing the extensive list of names of sugar (see Appendix I), it seemed wise to buy only products which contain only real, recognizable food ingredients. Imagine, you cannot even trust an ingredient called "natural flavors" because it is often sugar. When in doubt, I leave it out! Also, it is safer to buy products with a short list of ingredients. All presweetened products contain some form of sugar—usually maltodextrose, polydextrose or other sugars.

Under current labeling laws, sugar can still be hidden in many ways. On our zero-sugar food plan, we need to be aware of ingredients such as whey, natural flavors and fruit juice sweetener. Sugar by any other name is still sugar. Recovering food addicts need to seek products that are neither highly processed nor refined. Refined products, usually carbohydrates and sugars, trigger food addiction.

Diet Mentality

It is easy to spot the dieters in our midst. They talk about weight loss instead of recovery. They question the food plan and wonder whether they will lose weight "eating all that food." Because a characteristic of food addiction is obsession with weight, an important task of recovery is to change diet thinking so that we become recovery oriented rather than weight-loss oriented. The consequences of staying focused on weight loss will negatively affect recovery. If weight loss is the major reason one uses the food plan, recovery is not the goal. "Dieters" in the program tend to binge and restrict in order to maintain weight. They stay in the disease process and are not able to enter the recovery process. This is the disease of attitudes. Richard says, "If you focus on recovery, you will lose weight; if you focus on weight loss, you will lose recovery." That is the paradox! When our focus shifts from weight loss to recovery, we are finally able to get off the merry-go-round.

People-Pleasing

A people-pleaser is one who will do almost anything to keep from upsetting another person. A newcomer to recovery shared that she planned to eat lunch at a friend's home. She was unwilling to express her needs because it would be too "rude." Putting myself into the shoes of her hostess, I realized that I would feel terrible if someone had medical needs and I could have been helpful. Why would we want to put our health at risk in order to please someone else, whose opinion we don't even know? I have heard newcomers say that they just couldn't phone a sponsor because it would be such a bother.

These are core irrational beliefs that affect recovery: "I am not a worthwhile person;" "No one would love me as I am;" "I can control others;" and "I am responsible for others' feelings and behavior." The food addict typically has low self-esteem, is fearful of abandonment and is therefore willing to trade his or her needs for acceptance. A more healthy person would find this unacceptable.

Pam discussed her first attempt at recovery, saying, "My big mistake was that I was a people-pleaser and I would cave in just to keep the peace. If my recovery got in the way of my family's plans, I would drop my plan. I just didn't have the commitment, and in a way, I think that I didn't trust that recovery really works. I had a feeling that I couldn't do it. This second time around, I am making my stubborn streak work for me and I am willing to do everything. I do my recovery plan even when others don't like it." Pam dropped the excuses and is willing to go to any length to get it. If you don't think you are worth it, "act as if" you are.

Stuck in Guilt

"I feel guilty about my weight." "I feel guilty about what I have done to myself." "I feel guilty about all the diets that I went on and off." "I feel guilty about the money I spent on food, doctors and worthless weight-loss programs." On and on, we express our guilt about the disease. The reality is that we have a disease, we are not the disease. We inherited this disorder. It is not a question of will power or won't power, either. It is a biogenetic disease.

Guilt is a judgment we make upon ourselves. It has no value. Guilty thoughts produce toxic feelings that send us back to the food for relief. For some, the inventory process is guilt-provoking. How can we examine our past without falling into the guilt trap? Effective inventory is an objective evaluation as opposed to subjective judgment. We evaluate and correct our behavior rather than subjectively pass judgment upon ourselves. Here is an example of the difference between judgment and evaluation. Judgment says, "You were a bad person for eating too much. You should have done better." Evaluation says, "Overeating was not a recovery choice. I will discuss this with my sponsor and develop better ways to avoid making the decision to overeat again." Self-knowledge produces action and change rather than guilty feelings.

External Focus of Control

Those with an external focus of control look outside for solutions instead of inward. When we operate from this perspective, we lose touch with our inner signals. We believe that people, places and circumstances outside of ourselves have power over us. It seems that our happiness or pain is dependent on those outside circumstances. In recovery, we begin to take charge of our own lives. We no longer think: *If my spouse would only get a better job, everything would be all right.* Or, *If only my boss would leave me alone, I would be fine.* Or, *If my husband would get sober, I could stop overeating.* We no longer believe that if the right person were to do the right thing, we could be happy. We come to understand that happiness depends not on what happens, but what we do about it. Happiness is an inside job, when we become willing to be responsible for the quality of our lives.

Resentments Are the Number One Offender

The book *Alcoholics Anonymous* tells us: "Resentment is the 'number one' offender. It destroys more alcoholics than anything else." From our very earliest days in recovery, food addicts are told to "Work on your resentments if you want to stay abstinent!" What is a resentment? Resentment is score keeping. Remembering every old injury, hurt and wrong keeps us in the resentment. Usually we focus on certain people, while others can do no wrong. There are those whom we love to judge and blame and others who get off

scot-free. We go about proving our case when we start rant-
ing and raving about the person we resent–they are wrong,
we are right, they had better change! We usually find other
people who will agree with us and help us fan the flames
and keep the anger going.

Resentment is like drinking poison and thinking the
other guy will die. To rid ourselves of the poison, working
on our resentments is a priority task. Being willing to let go
of resentments in order to find peace, we list those whom
we resent during our inventory. Here is the process I use to
work through resentments:

- What did I want from the person I resent?
- Did I expect this person to act in a certain way?
- Did I blame this person when he or she did not meet
  my expectations?
- What is my error in this difficulty?
- Did I commit the error of judging, criticizing, expect-
  ing or blaming?
- Is maintaining this condition worth the pain it creates?
- How can I change this condition?

When we make demands on others, it fills us up with
toxic feelings of anger and resentment. Those demands take
us out of love, and we lose serenity. Our error creates pain.
The error is placing expectations, judgments, criticism and
blame on others. We can change our distressful condition
when we give up making demands on others. God's will,
not mine, be done. I change me, bless them and go forward
in peace and serenity. Finish with an affirmation: "I love and
accept [name the person you resented] just the way he or

she is today, because love and acceptance are spiritual principles and today I choose to live a spiritual way of life."

I'll Quit Tomorrow

As active food addicts, we were always planning to start
tomorrow or Monday or before the big occasion. "I will
start tomorrow," was our mantra. In recovery, we must
smash that mind-set. We come to realize that tomorrow
never comes. We must not put off good clean abstinence for
another day. Today is the only day we have. Commitment
to weighing and measuring, elimination of all addictive
foods, scheduling and good nutrition for this twenty-four
hours gives us a foundation to build on. Anything short of
doing the work of recovery will keep us in the disease.

Isolation

Isolation is a powerful barrier to recovery. In isolation we
avoid healthy relationships and practices such as attendance
at meetings and contact with our support people. These
contacts are important to continued success in recovery. A
food addict prone to isolation avoids phone calls, meetings
and the associations with recovering people that are critical
to his or her well-being. One food addict shares, "My program quickly degenerates when I miss meetings and ignore
phone calls. It doesn't take long for me to vegetate in front
of the TV. Switching on television seems to switch on my

obsession with food, too. That leads to overeating and binge eating of foods that are on the food plan. Of course, then volume is a problem."

What is going on when the food addict finds himself or herself in the isolation mode? Being home alone is the breeding ground for thoughts of food, which ultimately lead to overeating and binge eating. Isolation is a process of gradually eliminating recovery-related actions. Recovery is accomplished in relationships, including contact with a sponsor, telephone calls, meetings and step work. Withdrawing from these relationships is a definite sign of relapse. Once I asked a man about his recovery program. He said with great energy and enthusiasm, "Three phone calls a day, three meetings a week!" I knew he was on track, avoiding isolation and maintaining contact with his recovery network. We need to stay willing to let people into our lives.

Illness Stalls Recovery

It has been my observation that when recovering people get ill, often recovery disciplines are discarded. We miss phone calls, meetings and step work. Obviously illness puts us into a compromised position. You know how it goes: "I have been really sick with the flu and unable to eat all my food." I caution you to stay as close to the food plan as possible during bouts of illness. It requires every bit of discipline that we can muster to prepare and eat food when we don't feel like it. We need to remember that during a period of illness, food addiction does not go on hold. The disease is just as cunning, powerful and baffling as ever. So what can we do to maintain recovery during illness? Continue to make phone calls, ask for help with food preparation or shopping if necessary. Think of foods that will be appetizing during illness, because a certain food may be appealing or another may be horrible. Belief is a powerful tool. Believe that you can continue to recover even when feeling sick. Turn away from the idea that "I can't eat" and toward the idea that "I can stay on my food plan and my abstinence, no matter what!"

Stomach Upsets

It is tough to decide what to do about sticking to the food plan when we are sick, especially with stomach upsets. An upset stomach makes our usual foods seem so unappetizing. Unfortunately, restricting food puts recovery in jeopardy. Many relapses follow cases of stomach distress. It is very important to stick to the food plan as closely as possible and to eat as much food as we can tolerate. Maria reports, "When I had the flu last winter, I underate, and on some level I was so happy I would lose some weight. Then, after I began to feel better and tried to get back on my food plan, I overate. Looking back, I think I could have done much better with my food while I was sick, even though I was very sick. Actually, I ended up gaining some weight and struggling to get back to the food plan, so my 'diet' didn't work anyway."

Taking Medications

Many over-the-counter medications contain sugars. It is important to check labels. If the product only gives the active ingredients, you might assume that the inactive ingredients contain some form of sugar or starch, especially if it is in candy form. An alternative to using over-the-counter medications is the use of herbal teas for minor upsets. There are teas for the relief of congestion, stomach distress, flu and colds and more. Of course, it is important to check the label on medicinal teas, too. They may contain sweeteners. If you are seriously ill or your symptoms persist, consult your doctor. In this case it would be important to take the appropriate prescription. In the event that you will be using a prescription, inform the doctor about your need for medications free of sugar, starch and alcohol. Check with the pharmacist as well to double-check that your prescription medication will be safe for your sugar-free and wheat-free status.

12

Avoiding Relapse and Recognizing Relapse Warning Signs

Relapse Prevention and Treatment

Short-Term Gain, Long-Term Pain

Unlike barriers to recovery, which are characteristics of the disease process that we bring into recovery with us, relapse occurs after an effective program is in place. Relapse is a process of discarding effective recovery practices. Often food addicts return to binge or binge/purge behavior after short periods of abstinence. Food addiction relapse frequently features the "Zero-One" phenomenon, which entails doing Step Zero (relapse) and Step One (withdrawal) over and over so that the addict is always suffering in the disease or in withdrawal. With this pattern, there is never the opportunity to stabilize physically or to build strength in recovery because of frequent returns to active addiction. The disease provides short-term pleasure followed by long-term pain. Recovery provides short-term pain followed by long-term pleasure. The Zero-One relapser lives in the discomfort of both. Always in the pain of the disease or the pain of withdrawal, recovery cannot be too appealing to this type of relapser. It is too painful!

Other patterns of relapse occur over longer time spans. The recovering person develops a more enduring program of recovery lasting many weeks, months or years. Relapse occurs when the individual becomes complacent or overly confident, resulting in a process of decompensating in recovery. This involves the performance of increasingly more disease-related behaviors and fewer recovery-related tasks, until recovery is so weakened it can no longer withstand the power of the disease.

Most relapse occurs because the recovering person does not realize that such a phenomenon exists. It is deadly to miss the point that the key to all recovery is avoiding relapse. The major goals of relapse prevention are to evaluate personal relapse patterns, learn about the relapse process and develop an individualized plan to avoid it. It is a good idea to make a list of relapse warning signs and develop an intervention list. Interventions are those actions performed to counteract relapse symptoms. For instance, a relapse warning sign may be missing meetings. An intervention to counteract this symptom of relapse might be to make meeting attendance part of the daily commitment to our sponsor. In this way we become accountable for attending meetings.

It is important to know that relapse does not begin with the first bite of addictive substances. Instead, it is a spontaneous, usually unconscious process which ends with eating addictive substances. Recovery is based upon the conscious avoidance of relapse. We stop courting it. This is accomplished by "constant vigilance and awareness," as recommended in our recovery programs. Maintaining awareness of clean abstinence and an effective recovery program will serve to support continuing recovery and relapse avoidance. Our daily Tenth Step is the relapse prevention step. We use it to evaluate and correct our program on a daily basis.

It is difficult to recover and avoid relapse without good

information about both the disease process and the process of relapse. The surprising information is that, because recovering people cannot achieve perfect recovery, everyone who is in recovery is also in some stage of relapse. The key to continued recovery is to be aware of it in order to confront it in the early, weakest stage. Most food addicts relapse because they do not know how to prevent it. Relapse is like walking backward through the recovery process toward the disease, discarding recovery tools along the way. This process is complete when the person returns to the use of the addictive substance which triggers active disease. At this point, recovery and relapse end simultaneously as the disease takes over.

Mary's Relapse Story

Although recovery is threefold—physical, spiritual and mental—I find for me, I need to be secure in abstinence before I am able to look at the rest. As my significant other has said, "You are a scary and sick human being when you are in the food." Our relationship was almost destroyed by my recent year-long relapse. I had to move out of our house until I could get abstinent again. If I can remain abstinent for thirty more days and continue to go to meetings, use the telephone and do step work with my sponsor, I will be given a second chance, which is a miracle.

The destruction I have done while in relapse is immense and far-reaching. I have hurt myself, my family, my friends and others—while destroying my career, my finances and my health, as well as gaining back every one of the one hundred sixty-two pounds that I lost while abstinent. All this because I decided I wanted to eat sugar again and took one compulsive bite last November. If you are struggling with abstinence, you do not have to reach a bottom this low. You can stop the elevator when you want to get off badly enough—you do not have to go to the basement or depths of hell. I am being given a second chance at life, and for this I am grateful. I can't take the risk of losing everything again. I now choose to stay abstinent. It was hell getting it back this time, and it would only be worse if there was a next time. Thank God there is a solution. Just for today, I choose to be a part of it.

Relapse Warning List

You might like to make a list of your personal relapse warning signs. Here is a list developed by a sponsee. Her warning signs pertain to basic recovery disciplines. She says, "For me the following are warning signs of relapse":

1. When I do not eat my meals at the same time each day.
2. When I start thinking I can cut down food portions.
3. When I begin going out to eat on a regular basis.
4. When I find myself not wanting to eat my veggies.
5. When I start skipping meals.
6. When I am ashamed to take my measuring utensils into the restaurant.

7. When I stop doing my reading and writing assignments.
8. When I stop doing the steps and working the program.
9. When I stop going to meetings and making phone calls.
10. When I begin thinking, "I can do this on my own" and don't seek help.
11. When I make changes and refuse to report them to my food plan sponsor.

Relapse Traps

Customizing the Food Plan

The food plan is our prescription for recovery. The reported results of adherence to the plan are phenomenal, yet we want to make changes and adaptations. Unfortunately, when changes are made, balance is lost and negative consequences result. One food addict reports: "All I can say is that when I follow this plan to the letter, it works. If I don't, it won't. I was the queen of skipping meals or leaving out portions, and it took me into relapse again and again. I am a food addict. I may be intelligent, but this addiction is cunning, baffling, powerful and patient. I can't out-think it alone. I need to reach out to people in recovery who are doing the plan and follow it without alterations. My addictive mind wants me to customize so it can drag me back into the hell-hole of bingeing and purging. For me it is about surrender and about faith in this plan, which has worked for so many others."

Restricting

Skipping meals, reducing portion size or skipping portions is the fast track to relapse. Undereating is just as dangerous as overeating. After years of attempting restrictive diets, we become misled by the belief that "less is better" or that we are "good girls and boys" for eating less. Restricting sets us up to binge eat. The food plan is designed to maintain balance and equilibrium between hunger and satiety. It provides nutrients, fiber and fluids to ensure healthy bodily functioning. Our bodies use these nutrients to provide life energy.

In recovery we commit to providing our bodies what they need to operate efficiently—neither too much nor too little. This is accomplished by conscientious adherence to our food plan, regularly scheduled meals, careful measurement and planning ahead. So often meals or portions are missed due to lack of planning. Our food needs are so precise that failing to plan is definitely planning to fail. That devilish disease loves it when we do that!

Another issue is the complaint that "I can't eat all that food." The real question is, "You can't eat it or won't eat it?" It is important to maintain the portion size of the food plan in order to avoid hunger and eliminate craving. The plan is a low-fat, low-calorie, high-fiber food plan. The volume of fiber keeps us from experiencing hunger. Initially it seems like a very large amount of food, and it takes time for our digestive tract to get used to the volume of fiber. After all, we fed the disease with sticky, pasty, gooey, greasy foods that just slid right through our digestive tract. In recovery, we chew thoroughly, swallow and digest high-fiber foods.

Willingness to execute the food plan exactly the way it is written is a major key to recovery.

Increasing Volume

The other side of the coin is increasing volume. Lanie says, "My first sign of relapse is when I mound the cup." Volume problems may start with a simple-seeming decision to have a bit more. Gloria has "an extra glass of milk in the night, then a dish of oatmeal—and then it is off to the donuts!" Volume issues are resolved by using the cup, scale and measuring spoons—nothing more, nothing less.

Permission-Giving

The disease of food addiction speaks to us. The many lies it whispers in our ear usually lead to permission to weaken our program or to eat something "iffy." Such thoughts will lead us back into active addiction if not countered with rational and honest responses. At first these indulgent ideas look innocent. "Just doing myself a little favor—guess I'll stay home and relax tonight. I don't really need that meeting. Relaxation is good!" The good is the enemy of the best. Once permission is granted to forego a meeting, it becomes easier the next time to justify missing the meeting.

After the ball starts rolling, more allowances take place. "I can't get around to calling my sponsor." "It won't hurt to eat between meals." "I am too tired to do my Tenth Step; I will just watch TV instead." "It is okay to eat this food, it is not on the food plan but there is no sugar, flour or wheat in it.

I deserve a treat." "I will just eat this fruit now and not have one tonight before bed."

Permission-giving results in loss of the commitment which is critical to recovery. With each concession made to the disease, our programs are weakened and eventually destroyed. We need to respond when we hear something like this: "Surely it would be okay to have just one diet soda. Just one won't hurt." The response to such a permissive thought might go like this: "Caffeine and caramel color are not on my food plan for good reason. If it is all right to have them now, it would be all right to have them all the time. I will call my sponsor and discuss this idea with her." In this way we maintain the structure of our program and strengthen our resolve to maintain abstinent recovery.

Getting Too Tired

Healthy pursuits support good recovery, just as recovery supports good health. It is really important to develop a healthy lifestyle as our program evolves and to change unhealthy living habits which will undermine our growth and development. A major goal of recovery is to keep our brain chemistry in balance. An unhealthy lifestyle will keep it unbalanced instead, and we will be off looking for a way to feel better. We risk that it will be an addictive way to feel better by reaching for something mood altering.

Mary Beth says, "I have such a busy week at school that I sleep through my recovery meeting on Saturday morning. Other times I promise my sponsor I will be there but seldom make it." Adequate rest is really important to recovery.

Overwork, staying up too late watching television and drinking caffeine will all interfere with getting a good night's rest. Sometimes addicts want to "make up for lost time" and become overly involved in work, family and educational pursuits to the detriment of their recovery program. Getting too tired will lead to feelings of discouragement. After all, didn't we drag around feeling lethargic and tired all of the time while we were active in the disease? Real rest and real energy are gifts of recovery. We get adequate rest and relaxation so that we can enjoy and keep the gift of recovery.

Dishonesty

Recovery is built upon honesty. It is crucial to our recovery every step of the way, starting with an honest desire to stay abstinent, followed by an honest assessment of our physical, emotional, mental and spiritual decline in the disease, and maintained by honest evaluation of our daily behavior. If we return to our old dishonest ways, our recovery is threatened. It may start with a little white lie and build until we are back in the disease full time. Most relapse starts with lying about food. Dishonesty with weighing and measuring, lying about eating extra food or other ways of changing our food plan lead to relapse. We deceive our sponsors, our friends and families, but most importantly we deceive ourselves. The disease will produce all kinds of deceptions to lead us back into its downward progression. A daily program of identifying and correcting dishonesty that occurs in any area of our life is at the very core of life in recovery. The truth shall set us free! It is the way to break loose from the tyranny of food addiction.

Impatience, Frustration and Irritability

This unholy trio is spawned when things are not happening fast enough or others are not doing what we want. This is toe-tapping, finger-snapping time. Unsatisfied demands on others bring us no joy and keep us in a state of perpetual disturbance based on the belief that external circumstances create our happiness and satisfaction. Having expectations of others places us in a victim position. When our happiness becomes dependent on others doing our will, then impatience, frustration and irritability are produced. These are toxic conditions which will lead to anger and resentment and–if unchecked–relapse.

This revised version of the Serenity Prayer is an antidote to this condition: *God grant me the serenity to accept the person I cannot change, courage to change the person I can and wisdom to know that person is me.* I can only change myself; when it comes to others I let go and let God. *Bless them, change me.*

Need to Be Right

"I am right, you are wrong." These words have started every fight, war and argument known to man. Usually the idea is: "I am right, you are wrong and you had better change!" The need to be "right" is an ego mechanism. When I make irrational demands on others, it fills me with toxic feelings of anger, takes me out of love and I lose serenity.

In recovery we give up the fight. We begin to recognize that opinions differ and others have the right to their own ideas. Eventually we realize that we can change only what we ourselves think, say and do. Everything else is beyond our control. By using the slogan, "Live and Let Live," we suspend judgment, criticism and control and allow others to manage their own lives while we attend to our own inventories. Choose peace over power.

Self-Pity

Feeling sorry for ourselves can take us into the emotional basement and possible relapse very quickly. Poor me, poor me, pour me a milk shake! We create our own sadness, unhappiness and discontentment. Self-pity cuts us off from communication with God and the people in our lives due to our outrageous demands and unreasonable expectations. In the self-pity mode, we are ever critical, never satisfied or grateful. This is a piercingly painful condition, and we do not usually understand that we are creating it all on our own.

Betty says, "I was full of pain and anguish, feeling sorry for myself because things weren't going my way. I was making outside people, places and things responsible for my contentment. I was so sick of the pain, I dropped to my knees and asked to be changed. With my sponsor, studying the steps and continued prayer, I worked my way out of the pain. I learned to be grateful." Start with a gratitude list. That is an effective antidote for self-pity. Writing five things that we are grateful for on a daily basis is an effective program of recovery from self-pity.

Complacency

I've got it made, Kathleen thought. She figured since she had gone to treatment, she would never relapse, because she saw others doing so well after treatment. "Binge eating was the furthermost thing from my mind," she said. On the other hand, recovery was no longer a dominant thought, either. It was dangerous to let up on recovery disciplines just because everything was going well. Sometimes relapses occur when things are great. The interesting fact of recovery is that we either grow or go. My old friend Charlie used to say, "I'd rather be green and growing than ripe and rotten." Letting up on disciplines such as prayer, meditation, daily inventory and meeting attendance indicates complacency. This is a luxury we cannot afford; the cost of relapse is too great.

Expectations of Others

Marcella called her sponsor and asked, "I've changed; why hasn't anyone else?" Her sponsor replied, "It would be a plus if they would, but why make it a problem if they do not? They may not trust you yet, or they may still be looking for further proof of your recovery. You cannot expect others to change their style of life just because you have." When it comes to our friends, family members and other close associates, we have to understand that they don't understand. Look at how long it took for us to be converted to a recovery way of life. We cannot place expectations on our loved ones to change, too. Work to change the world and nothing happens, change yourself and the world changes. Accept them and change me as the Serenity Prayer instructs.

Rebellion

This seems to be a built-in aspect of addiction. That we rebel against the discipline of recovery is not surprising, because historically addicts are rule breakers. Oftentimes it feels like we come kicking and screaming into recovery. Laurie explains that she just doesn't want to weigh and measure her food. She says, "I am just rebellious, I guess. I don't want to do that!" But what are we rebelling against? It seems as though we are rebelling against our own best interest. When rebellion weakens our resolve to practice recovery disciplines, recovery is compromised. Fanny says, "I think rebellion is always the bottom line whenever I have a slip. I am just throwing a tantrum and saying 'No–I won't!' Now it doesn't always have to be obvious. I am a master at the passive/aggressive stuff. But deep down I start playing those tapes that say 'It's not fair,' and 'I'm going to get as much as everybody else!' I also notice a lot of self-pity and sadness along with the anger when I rebel. For some reason it hurts deep down inside that I have to do things differently, and it reinforces the feeling of being different that I have suffered from all my life."

We rebel against the perception that we are being controlled. "No matter how good my program was, there was always a part of me rebelling against anyone external telling me what to do," says Judy. Actually that is a false perception; the truth is, no one really tells us what to do. In recovery, we just share our experience, strength and hope with each other. We see the solution to our addiction as a set of rules and regulations rather than the way out. One of Fanny's issues is that she tells herself she can't have something that will harm her. When we tell ourselves we can't have or do something, we are likely to rebel against that idea. "Don't tell me what I cannot have, what I cannot do!" The truth is that we can have that item. We can have anything we want if we are willing to pay the price. When we *choose* not to have something harmful, it becomes a choice rather than a command. That is what recovery is–a choice.

Emotional Relationships

Many years ago, when I first came into recovery, the wise saying was, "No emotional involvement in the first year." The reasoning behind this was that, in the early years of recovery, time is spent stabilizing. A passionate relationship is risky business, for it will tend to destabilize the new person. When young women asked me to sponsor them I would make a point by saying, "Sure, until you get a boyfriend. When you get one, call me. I will want to resign." I knew the roller-coaster ride would start with a new relationship, beginning with euphoria and usually ending in pain and disillusion. These strong feelings are too much for the emotionally immature newcomer. This must have been the case in the early years, when one of the old-timers was quoted as saying, "When the redhead walks in, recovery walks out!"

Other Addictions

It is important to be aware that other addictions affect our recovery from food addiction. Whether or not we are able to address all of our addictions at once, it is advisable to understand that other addictions may progress when we start abstaining from addictive food substances. For instance, many recovering food addicts discover that compulsive spending quickly escalates after starting abstinence. Then, too, when we come into recovery, we already may be established in other addictive processes such as smoking or prescription drug abuse. Sometimes these are called "substitute addictions," but actually they are full-blown addictions. Apologies for finger pointing, but we do see recovering alcoholics smoking, eating sweets and drinking caffeine at meetings. Food addicts talk of spending sprees, caffeine and nicotine use, relationship addictions and other compulsions springing up after abstinence. It is important to admit to these addictions and to be willing to address them when the time is right. For some of us it takes years to become ready to get into recovery from other addictions, for others it all happens in a fairly brief period of time. It takes recognition, admission, acceptance and action—one addiction at a time!

Overdoing

Andy shares, "In addiction, I stayed on the couch—miserable, gaining weight, depressed and negative. After I got abstinent, I went to the other extreme and got overly active. Then I ended up back on the couch. This is a pattern

I have recognized, and I am beginning to see my need to learn 'Easy does it.'" Sometimes we believe that we need to play catch-up by correcting all of the errors of our years in the disease by getting as much done as soon as possible. We overhaul the house, take on a part-time job, go to ninety meetings in ninety days and take a few college courses on the side. Overdoing can take the form of perpetual motion. When we stop bingeing on food, it is possible we might start bingeing on work or busyness. This can be another way of avoiding facing ourselves. This behavior results in exhaustion, resentment and dissatisfaction. Hopefully, we find a way to correct overdoing before it takes us back into the food for relief.

"Awfulizing" Recovery and Euphoric Recall of Addiction

Recently I received a message on the Internet that bemoaned all the work it took to achieve abstinent recovery: cooking, planning, meetings, step work and all the rest. Negativity is pretty easy for us—we have a history of negative thinking. "Awfulizing" is negative self-talk that makes our situation in recovery appear to be unbearable while making the disease look inviting. Awfulizing is usually coupled with euphoric recall of the disease, which is fond memories of the affliction. Feedback from friends and sponsors shows us that the work of recovery results in some pretty terrific payoffs, while the disease still results in severely negative consequences. As with all kinds of negative thinking, a gratitude list will get things back into perspective.

After the Test, I Crash!

"It seems like I am able to do really well when it comes to the most stressful situations, whether it is a big party, trip, family get-together or work assignment. During the crisis I am very cautious about my food plan. Then I breathe a sigh of relief and when it is all over–I relapse!" This familiar story was told yet again this week by a young woman who had maintained abstinence during a trip out of the country. The bad news was that she returned to binge food shortly after returning home. After evaluating her behavior during the time that she was out of the country, it became apparent that the only thing she did during the trip was the food plan. She stopped contacting her sponsor, attended no meetings, discontinued her step work and relied only on the food plan for her recovery. She stopped recovering and started dieting.

The food plan without a program is a diet. We cannot stay abstinent on yesterday's program. And we can't stay on diets at all. In order to maintain a stable recovery, we must determine how to keep our program active on a daily basis. Some combination of meetings, phone calls, sponsor contact, step work, prayer and meditation is necessary to maintain recovery. The problem with demanding situations is that often the focus is shifted from recovery to the matter at hand and recovery is no longer a priority. Recovery is either first or zero–it cannot be relegated to second place.

13

Recovery Challenges for Special Populations and Situations

Underweight and Addicted to Food

Often underweight food addicts purge or restrict. Coming into recovery with underweight status can present particular challenges. Sometimes the smaller person hears such things in the recovery rooms as: " I don't know what is wrong with you, but you don't belong here." One purging bulimic who heard those words says, "The next time I went to a meeting, I was obese." We can only guess the person who said those words to her was there to lose weight, not to recover. We know that food addicts come in all sizes and shapes, from emaciated to morbidly obese and everything in between. The common factor with all food addicts is loss of control over food, not one's current weight.

Along the same lines: "It is hard to identify if there is a lot of 'weight-loss talk' in the rooms," says one low-weight food addict. "That is not my issue. I want to learn safe, guilt-free eating and how to find my way out of this disease. Talk about the Twelve Steps and I am all ears."

Another challenge for an underweight person is eating the amount of food prescribed by the food plan. We hear such laments as, "I can't eat all that food! I will gain weight!" It is crucial to overcome this block to recovery. First of all, the food is high in fiber, low in calories and low in fat. It is designed to nourish the body while eliminating cravings caused by more processed, calorie-dense foods. Since the plan is low in fat, something is required to maintain satisfaction and freedom from hunger. That is the fiber in the food plan. Eliminate the fiber by reducing the volume of food, and hunger is the result. Unnecessary hunger sets up the next binge. Reducing the amount of food in the plan is practicing the disease by continuing to restrict.

It is also important for the underweight person who has purged to put the digestive tract back into operation in the intended way: ingestion, digestion and elimination. Purgers skip the digestive process by inducing vomiting. Since most purgers eat high-fat and high-carbohydrate foods that are easy to eliminate by induced vomiting, their digestive tracts operate inefficiently. Laxatives and diuretics also take their toll on physical well-being and healthy elimination. It is a big step to learn to trust the food plan, to follow directions and to put the digestive tract back into action. Those who are willing to do this will find recovery.

Men Are Food Addicted, Too

There are some myths and issues affecting men who are food addicted that require examination, such as, "Eating disorders are not manly," and "Food is a woman's issue." Over the years we may have been tempted to believe that food addiction was a female disease. The majority of people who came to recovery meetings and treatment programs were women. The truth is, males are addicted to food, too. We don't know the numbers yet, but they are probably equal in number. An enabling attitude that keeps men in the disease is that "It is fine for men to be big." This irrational concept focuses on size and ignores the health risks of food addiction. Just think of how many football players and other massive-weight sports figures suffer when the games are over. Sane thinking dictates that we think of food addiction as a dangerous disease. And, despite the requirements of any sport, health is compromised by out-of-control eating.

Some say, "Men can't identify with those women at Twelve-Step meetings." It was the same for women in AA years ago, when there were a few uncomfortable women at meetings with great numbers of men. No wonder alcoholism has been considered the men's addiction and food addiction the women's. In food addiction recovery groups, men have played the minority role, attending meetings with many women. Twelve-Step programs are just as effective for men as for their female counterparts. With some minor portion adjustments to the food plan, men use the same tools of recovery as women. Yes, we do see many women in our recovery programs, but in parts of the country where men are active in recovery, we see increasingly larger numbers of men at meetings.

"I don't know how to cook!" Some men do not know how to cook and therefore do not know how to manage the food plan. This is an issue that needs problem-solving. There are many ways to get around it. Some men learn how to cook, others have relatives who do it for them, while others learn how to make restaurant eating work for them.

"My wife won't cooperate." It would be great if our loved ones would fall in line and demonstrate complete cooperation and support. In order to recover, a food addict needs scheduled meals, and the food plan requires planning, shopping, cooking and cleaning up. All of this takes time and energy. Some wives are not willing to accept responsibility for these tasks. From time to time, we realize that someone's spouse may be food addicted, too. It is understandable that, in such a situation, the wife might be threatened by the husband's recovery. She may not be ready to get into recovery herself. One wife of a recovering food addict told me, "It was like he changed the rules. We ate together for all of our married life and then he got on this food plan. I really resented it! There was an implication that I should change my eating, too. I was not ready to do that." If this is the case, the food addict himself must accept responsibility for food management if he is to enjoy recovery.

Young People in Recovery

Children in recovery need parents who are willing to go to any length to support them. We are not saying parents who are willing to go to any length to force them! The prerequisite for recovery is the child's willingness to take the necessary actions. Brannin, a teenager in recovery, is an example of this. He says that he wanted to play sports, but due to his childhood obesity he could not run. When running, he was quickly out of breath. In a small group of recovering kids, there was consensus on this subject. They all wanted to be able to run. Food addiction was keeping them from doing sports and running around with the other kids.

With his parents' cooperation and his brother's, too,

Brannin has stayed motivated to maintain two and a half years of abstinence from ages fourteen to sixteen. He is willing to go to any lengths to stay on his food plan. He says, "Many times the other guys have a fast-food dinner that costs a few dollars while my abstinent food costs twice as much! I will spend the extra money in order to stay abstinent. And sometimes it is a pain, getting the food I need." One time his girlfriend offered him something off his plan. He told her that if he ate it, it would not be long before she would no longer want to be his friend.

It is hard for young children and adolescents to be different from their peers. An eight-year-old girl who decided she was sick of being tired all the time went on the food plan. The first time she attended a going-away party for a classmate at school, she said: "It was so hard, but while the others were having cake I collected autographs in a book for the girl who was leaving. I didn't want to be sick and tired from that cake." Brannin's mother showed up at school for one of his parties with a fruit cup for every classmate. He was able to participate and didn't feel different. He says, "Mom has been spectacular, magnificent in her support of my abstinence. She gives me money for my meals, gets up and fixes my breakfast and packs my abstinent lunches."

The first priority for a child on the food plan is to get the approval of the pediatrician. An obese six-year-old child's doctor was delighted that she was willing to improve her eating and supported the use of the food plan. That little girl worked hard to find food she would enjoy on the food plan. Although she loudly lamented the loss of her favorite binge food, she shopped diligently to find food she might like.

Of course, youngsters experience withdrawals, too. Brannin tells us, "The first month is the hardest, going through withdrawal. After that, it has been great."

More Than One Hundred Pounds Overweight

Those who have over a hundred pounds to lose have special challenges. Eileen shared with me that in her first go-around in recovery her focus on weight loss weakened her recovery. After an eight-year relapse, she has taken another approach in her current recovery. With a current six-year record of continuous recovery, she shares what she learned from her earlier experience. She says, "My weight loss tipped the scales in more ways than one!" As she lost over a hundred and fifty pounds, she became the local recovery celebrity, getting many compliments. She felt "high and elated" about her weight loss and the attention she was getting. As people got used to her size-eight figure, she lost her celebrity status. She started to feel disappointed because her expectations were not being met. She said, "I wasn't getting the gold medals I expected from the people around me." She expected that weight loss would make her happy and realized too late that thin is not necessarily well. This time around, she uses her scale to weigh and measure her food and abstains from weighing her body. She says, "For me, it is important to focus on recovery instead of weight loss."

Eileen also felt protected from her sexuality by being obese. Weight loss left her in a vulnerable place. Using the

Twelve Steps and her recovery program, she is adjusting to her new body image and sexuality. As a chronic food addict in advanced stages of the disease, Eileen says, "I had so much work to do when I came into recovery it was overwhelming. The destruction to my mental and physical health, my family and my environment was enormous. The magnitude of the destruction kept me in the disease. I had so much repair work to do. In order to recover, I had to name my task for the day and complete one task at a time. Slowly but surely, the destruction is being remedied."

Addicted to Exercise

"One of the hardest and the best things I have ever done is give up a bicycle marathon to raise money for breast cancer research," says Millie. "My mother died of breast cancer, and I wanted to participate in that bike-a-thon in her memory. I had been planning it for a long time. I went into treatment for food addiction, and both a doctor and a therapist in group confronted me for planning to do this in my first month out of treatment." Millie came to realize that the physical effort of training and the marathon itself would not only stress and detract from her newly found recovery, but would stress the caloric limits of her food plan. Her food plan had been developed for moderate levels of exercise plus moderate daily activity. It would not be appropriate for the level of activity of a bicycle marathon. Millie says, "I put my health first and found another way to express my love for my mother."

The carbohydrate loading necessary for athletics and

extreme exercise programs is inappropriate for food addicts who are carbohydrate sensitive. We suggest that those who participate in more than forty-five minutes to one hour of exercise adjust their exercise program rather than adjust the food plan. This is putting "first things first."

For food-addicted exercise addicts, exercise appears to be a "good thing." They argue eloquently to maintain their current level of extreme exercise, not realizing that this is another way to purge as a response to binge eating. Mary Ellen says, "I would often exercise way beyond what my exercise physiologist recommended. I would always find the time, money and energy to exercise in order to avoid the guilt and fear caused by my binge eating." She would take any opportunity to exercise—for instance, stretching while others in the room were relaxing, reading or watching television. In recovery she makes a daily commitment to her sponsor to limit exercise to an agreed-upon daily time period. Early in recovery she had to abstain from exercise altogether. The greatest challenge for exercise bulimics who wish to recover is to adjust exercise to meet their recovery needs.

Vegetarians

We are often asked about developing a vegetarian food plan. One problem associated with a vegetarian diet is that vegetable forms of protein such as beans and tofu deliver both protein and carbohydrate. Carbohydrate is our drug of choice. The metabolism of protein is favorable to our brain chemistry. The recovery food plan has been designed based on a beneficial balance between protein and carbohydrate. To develop a vegetarian food plan by increasing the carbohydrate content of the food plan and decreasing protein, it diminishes the effectiveness of the plan. For this reason, we continue to advise against vegetarian diets. Many people have been successful eating one vegetarian meal per day while continuing to incorporate fish, chicken and dairy products in the remaining meals.

An associated issue is that of juicing. Let's look at the danger of this practice for a moment. Juicing eliminates fiber and uses concentrated carbohydrate and liquid residue. It takes many vegetables and fruits to produce one cup of juice. Juicing discards the measurements recommended in the recovery food plan. The practice of juicing also is contrary to one of the basic elements of our successful food plan. We have created a high-fiber approach to abstinence. The recovery food plan is dependent on the high-fiber content to keep us satisfied, which is very different from the satiety achieved by high-fat diets. To do away with this friendly fiber by juicing also eliminates the important high-fiber elements of the food plan and leaves us wondering why we are hungry and craving.

The last concern about vegetarian eating plans is that they reduce choices. This affects variety. Those who choose among vegetable and animal protein have many choices. Those who choose only vegetable protein have far fewer options. Limited choices lead to boredom and possible allergies. Having said this, we do have faith that someday someone will find a vegetarian way to abstinence. So far we have not found a safe alternative to the recovery food plan.

We stand ready to examine a safe vegetarian approach that can be replicated.

Pregnant and Nursing Moms

Pregnant and nursing moms who prioritize recovery based on a food plan also prioritize their health and the health of their children. To continue to use sugar and refined carbohydrates addictively during pregnancy and nursing subjects the fetus and newborn to the same physiological and emotional swings that the mother experiences. This results in an agitated mother and an agitated child. When the flight attendant at the beginning of a flight tells parents to take care of their oxygen needs first and then attend to children, I always think of the recovering parent. It is so tempting to put the child's needs first while downplaying personal survival needs. Instead, putting recovery needs first improves the chances that the child will have a healthy, nurturing parent.

What is the food plan for a pregnant and nursing mom? Check with your doctor first. Many doctors approve of the recovery food plan. Others may want particular adjustments. Work with your sponsor or a nutritionist who is familiar with abstinence-based recovery. It is important when adjusting the food plan for special needs to maintain the balance between protein and carbohydrate, to eliminate addictive trigger foods, to maintain a balanced metabolism by regularly scheduled meals and to manage volume by weighing and measuring.

Lactose Intolerance

This is a subject dear to the author's heart. For more than seventeen years, I suffered from diarrhea, intense pain, gas and the expense of many inaccurate diagnoses. Then I discovered from a health book that I had symptoms of lactose intolerance. The same article that described the symptoms offered a treatment approach: eliminate all dairy products except yogurt. On the first day of this regimen I felt better, on the second day I felt even better and on the third day the symptoms were gone entirely. They were never to return, except on one occasion when I had regular skim milk in decaf coffee. I have added lactose-reduced milk to my food plan as well as yogurt. Sometimes in place of the dairy serving, I have two ounces of protein. This slight adjustment in my food plan has resulted in pain-free living.

Religious Observances

When religious observances seem to be in conflict with recovery principles, it has been my experience that compromises and concessions to good health are often worked out. It is important to explain recovery to our spiritual advisors. It is critical for them to understand that adherence to a recovery plan is an issue of health and sanity. Usually the recovering person is given a dispensation from fasting and other practices which may interfere with recovery. Fasting, which creates metabolic imbalance, is especially dangerous for food addicts. Food restriction is the fast track to binge eating, which may lead to addictive eating. On the other hand, abstinence from meat is easily accomplished by substituting fish and eggs for meat. Kosher dairy and meat restrictions are also easily remedied. Protein for metabolic balance following a meat meal is an acceptable alternative to dairy. Drinking wine, grape juice or eating bread as part of religious observances also have come into question. This concern has been worked out in various ways, from taking minuscule amounts to abstinence from these practices. It is a good idea to look for people in good recovery who have found satisfactory answers to our questions concerning religious practices.

14

The Payoffs:
The Blessings
and Benefits
of Recovery

So there it is! Ideas for those who are tired of being pushed around by food. There are lots of suggested practices proven to aid in recovery from food addiction. We don't have to do them all at once. The best idea is to formulate a simple, "do-able" program that works. We have to walk a fine line between "too much" and "not enough." Once I heard a man say that if he had to stay abstinent the way Joe did it, he wouldn't make it. That is the beauty of recovery–it is individualized.

No matter what, recovery requires focus, time, energy and effort. We never want to forget that the disease took more. The choice is ours every day. We can choose to medicate and ignore our spiritual work, or we can do our spiritual work and stop medicating.

So what's the payoff? As Annuncia says, "I am not crashed out asleep on the couch every night in a carbo fog–my head feels a little clearer. My car is cleaner without all those crumbs! My mood is stable, rather than being in a teary, highly depressed state over the least little thing. This is by far the most important positive change for me; I could not live like that anymore. When I eat now I am satisfied, not wanting more of something. I am not hungry all the time. I have met some wonderful, insightful, supportive people going through the same thing. I am caring about myself a little more."

We weigh what we give up against the gifts of recovery. Since we give up just one bite of binge food–the first one– it looks like recovery wins!

Gratitude is an amazing and powerful component of

recovery. I once saw this demonstrated vividly with Sandy, one of my clients. I could actually see her move out of self-pity and into happiness when she said, "Lucky me, I am so blessed!" Her whole affect and demeanor changed. The whole atmosphere of the room was transformed.

I love the following statement on gratitude, author unknown: "The opposite of pride is not humility, as we might think, but gratitude. The best antidote for resentments is making a gratitude list, concentrating on the person, or incident, you're resentful about. If you resent something your spouse did, make a gratitude list about all the good things your spouse does. The best antidote for anger is making a gratitude list. The best antidote for self-pity is, guess what? Making a gratitude list."

Here is Alan's gratitude list in reverse order:

This is my top ten list of positive consequences after eight months of recovery, abstinence and a loss of one hundred eleven pounds:

10. My clothing always fits—I'm in no danger of dying by strangulation.

9. The comments I get from people are so funny I laugh all day.

8. I really love those comments from women—I never get tired of hearing "You look great!"

7. I can shop at "real" people stores, not just at "Big and Tall" shops.

6. I've read a lot of really good books by brilliant, insightful, recovering authors about recovery and my religion.

5. My blood pressure has dropped from 150/110 to 130/82.

4. "Willpower" has become irrelevant. I follow the prescribed food plan, which is in black and white, nothing in between.

3. I have way more freedom to live my life because I don't have to dwell on food all the time.

2. I deal with life's problems and emotions as they come up—I don't use food to solve anything.

1. And the number one positive consequence of recovery and abstinence: I can look my children, wife, mom and dad in the eyes and know I am not going to die early from food addiction.

Once we begin living life on life's terms, we begin to see that life isn't all that bad. Life without the drug is actually pretty good. Addiction created the nightmare. We ate addictively to numb the feelings that were created by the addiction. What a rip-off! And we stayed stuck in our old patterns. Recovery shows us how to get unstuck, break our old patterns and enjoy new ways of living. Judy Z. recognizes that her recovery is physical, mental and spiritual. She says, "I am feeling better, loving myself again and knowing the real me. My weight loss is awesome, but the fact that I can work through feelings without using food to numb them is even more awesome. Now I feel the feelings. Sometimes it is so hard, but it is worth it in the end. My relationship with God is better. The bottom line is dealing with life without that drug (food) to numb and stuff my body so I don't have to feel. Now I am in tune with my body."

Some families benefit on different levels when the addict is more stable. According to Judy M., "My marriage is so much better! Prior to starting the program five months ago, my husband was pretty disgusted with me and my weight gain, bingeing behavior, mood swings and anger. Now he smiles a lot more (especially at me!), acts attracted to me again and wants to do more family activities. It's wonderful! Of course, I feel better, too: clearheaded, calmer (most of the time!), more energetic, less body aches and pains, and I even lost my PMS! I'm more patient with my five-year-old, which she loves! And I'm much more productive at work, and I've gone from part-time to a demanding full-time job without feeling overwhelmed."

Robin S. also has a better relationship with her husband as the result of her recovery efforts. "Now I feel clearheaded instead of drugged and hungover from sugar. I am able to be present in my relationship with my husband instead of obsessing and planning my next binge or feeling guilty about my last one. I am learning that I'm not the only person in the whole world who feels and acts the way I do. Now I have much more time and money, which was formerly spent on food and bingeing."

I often laugh at the joke, "Of all the things I've lost, I miss my mind the most!" Cynthia C. missed hers, too: "The best thing I find as a positive consequence of recovery on this food plan is clarity of thinking. Food is no longer an option in my decision-making process. It feels so clean, so right. With my abstinence program and the Twelve Steps, I have a program for great living!"

Diane has long-term recovery. I asked about her life in

recovery. She shared with me that "the tasks stay exactly the same as they were from day one. I haven't had alcohol, sugar or starches since March 17, 1984. I abstain from caffeine, and I quit smoking. I eat three meals a day, weighed or 'eyeballed,' with a snack at night. I have a sponsor and go to meetings. I am on my knees every night and morning. I am with people who are in recovery a great deal of the time. I help whenever I am asked—sometimes even when I am not asked! I read *One Day at a Time*. I am on the alert all the time. Before I get out of bed in the morning, I make a food plan up for the day. If I get too unsure, I submit my plan to a friend. Just like at the beginning, there are times when I feel that there is not enough food or it is not coming fast enough. God is taking care of me now as he did in the beginning."

As the result of this program, Diane says, she has "more balance in my life. I am still angry, lonesome, fearful, untrusting of other people and not believing that good things will happen to me. All the hurtful feelings are still there, but they are the weakest part of my personality now. They don't rule—they are diminished. Today I can be the thoughtful, kind, fun, spontaneous person I was as a child. What a joy that childlike person is to me. The fact that I know there are answers to my problems and where to find those answers is the great gift of recovery. It is the gift I am giving to my daughter. I have found peace, joy and love."

And so it is!

Appendix I

Hidden Sugars

**Names of Sugars, Alcohol Sugars, Fruit Sugars
and Sugar Products
(List developed by Barbara Caravella, CNC)**

Ace K (found in soda)
Acesulfame-k (Sunette, Sweet and Safe, Sweet One)
Alcohol sugars ("ol" endings–sorbitol, mannitol, etc.)
Amasake
Apple sugar
Artificial sweetener packets (Equal, Sweet 'n Low, etc.)
Artificial flavors (Call the company about the product
    contents.)
Aspartame/NutraSweet (causes cravings, made from
    alcohol sugar)
Augmiel
Bakery products
Barbados sugar
Bark sugar (also called Zylose)
Barley malt
Barley syrup
Beer/alcohol drinks
Beet sugar
Black strap molasses

Breath fresheners (Read the label for added sugars.)
Brown rice syrup
Brown sugar
Brown sugar syrup
Candy
Cane juice
Cane sugar
Carbitol
Caramel coloring
Caramel sugars
Caramelized sugar (Used in restaurants by heating
 sucrose until it browns.)
Canned foods (Look for sugar in vegetables, fruits,
 soups, beans, etc.)
Carob chips/powder
Cereals (made with added sugar)
Chewing gum
Chocolate
Ciders
Cocoa
Colorose
Concentrated fruit juice
Confectioners sugar
Corn sweetener
Corn syrup
D-tagatose
Dark brown sugar
Date sugar
Dextrin
Dextrose

Diglycerides

Disaccharides

Dried/dehydrated fruit (figs, raisins, apple chips, etc.)

Drinks (all soda pop, fruit drinks, alcoholic drinks, etc.)

Evaporated cane juice

Extracts (any type or flavor)

Florida crystals (evaporated cane juice)

Frozen yogurt/tofutti

Fructooligosaccharides (FOS)

Fructose

Fruit flavorings (Call the company about the product
    contents.)

Fruit juice (Call the company for added or hidden
    sugar.)

Fruit juice concentrate

Galactose

Glucitol

Glucoamine

Glucose

Glucose polymers

Glucose syrup

Glycerides

Glycerine

Glycerol

Glycol

Granulated sugar

Grape sugar

High fructose corn syrup

Honey (any type or form)

Ice cream/sorbet/frozen yogurt

Inversol
Invert sugar
Isomalt
Jaggery
Jams/jellies
Lactose
Levulose
Light brown sugar
"Light" sugar
"Lite" sugar
"Low" sugar
Malted barley
Maltitol
Malto (any)
Maltodextrins
Maltodextrose
Maltose
Malts (any)
Mannitol
Mannose
Maple sugar
Maple syrup
Marinades (Read the label on the product and be careful with meats in restaurants.)
Microcrystalline cellulose
Milled sugar
Modified food starch (added into dairy products)
Molasses
Monoglycerides
Monosaccharides

Monosodium glycerides
"Natural" flavors (Call the company for product contents.)
Natural milled cane sugar
"Natural" sugar (Call the company for product contents.)
"Natural" sweeteners
"Naturally" sweetened
Nectars
Neotame
Olestra (made from sucrose)
"OSE" (any: sucrose, dextrose, fructose, etc.)
Pentose
Polydextrose
Polyglycerides
Powdered sugar
Power/sports/nutrition/energy bars
Presweetened products
Processed meats (deli meats, cold cuts, hot dogs, etc.)
Raisin juice
Raisin paste
Raisin syrup
Raw sugar
Ribose
Rice malt
Rice sugar
Rice sweeteners
Rice syrup
Rice syrup solids
Saccharides (any)

Sauces (check label and/or call company)
Shakes/powdered/sports/nutrition drinks
Soda/soft drinks
Sorbitol (also called Hexitol)
Sorghum
Splenda (Sucralose)
Stevia (causes cravings)
Sucanat (evaporated cane juice)
Sucralose
Sucrose
Sugarcane
Sugar cubes
"Sugar-free" products
Sunette/Sweet-One (Acesulfame-k)
Sweet Thing (contains Aspartame and other sugars)
Sweetener 2000/NutraSweet 2000
Syrups (any)
Table salt (Read the label for added dextrose.)
Table sugar
Trisaccharides
Turbinado sugar
Unrefined sugar
Vanillan
Whey (71 percent sugar; avoid if it is added into a product)
White sugar
Xanthum gum (called corn sugar gum, fermented in
    corn sugar)
Xylitol
Yinnie syrup
Zylose

Appendix II

Forms of Flour and Flour Products

(List developed by Barbara Caravella, CNC)

Almond flour
Amaranth flour
Bagels
Bakery products
Barley flour
Blue corn chips
Blue corn flour
Bread products
Buckwheat flour
Chestnut flour
Corn chips
Corn flour
Cornmeal
Cottonseed flour
Crackers (any)
Enriched bleached flour
Enriched wheat flour
Malted barley flour
Millet flour
Multi-grain flour

Nacho chips
Noodles
Oat flour
Pasta (any)
Pastry flour
Pea flour
Pita bread
Pizza
Polenta (cornmeal)
Potato flour
Pretzels
Processed cereals (Made with sugar, flour and wheat)
Quinoa flour
Rice flour
Rye flour
Sago flour
Semolina flour
Sesame flour
Sorghum flour
Soy flour
Spelt flour
Spinach flour
Tapioca flour
Teff flour
Tortillas/tacos
Triticale flour
Wheat flour
White flour
Whole-grain bread
Yam flour

Names of Wheat and Wheat Products

Bagels

Bakery products

Bran (made from wheat)

Bread products (made from wheat)

Bulgur

Couscous

Cracked wheat

Crackers

Durum

Grape nuts

Gluten (wheat protein)

Kamut

Noodles

Pastas

Pizza

Pretzels

Processed cereals

Processed meat products (may contain wheat; check label)

Red wheat

Red spring wheat

Semolina

Shoyu sauce

Shredded wheat

Soy sauce

Spelt

Veggie burgers (may contain wheat; check label)

Wheat berries

Wheat bran
Wheat flakes
Wheat germ
Wheat gluten
Wheat grass
Wheat grass juice
Whole-grain wheat
Winter wheat

Appendix III

Why Sugar Is Dangerous

Here are 87 reasons why sugar and sweeteners are ruinous to health, from the book *Lick the Sugar Habit* by Nancy Appleton, Ph.D. Reprinted with permission of the author.

1. Sugar can suppress the immune system.
2. Sugar upsets the minerals in the body.
3. Sugar can cause hyperactivity, anxiety, difficulty concentrating and crankiness in children.
4. Sugar can produce a significant rise in triglycerides.
5. Sugar contributes to the reduction in defense against bacterial infection.
6. Sugar can cause kidney damage.
7. Sugar reduces high density lipoproteins.
8. Sugar leads to chromium deficiency.
9. Sugar leads to cancer of the breast, ovaries, prostate and rectum.
10. Sugar can increase fasting levels of glucose.
11. Sugar causes copper deficiency.
12. Sugar interferes with absorption of calcium and magnesium.
13. Sugar can weaken eyesight.

14. Sugar raises the level of a neurotransmitter called serotonin.
15. Sugar can cause hypoglycemia.
16. Sugar can produce an acidic stomach.
17. Sugar can raise adrenaline levels in children.
18. Sugar malabsorption is frequent in patients with functional bowel disease.
19. Sugar can cause aging.
20. Sugar can lead to alcoholism.
21. Sugar can cause tooth decay.
22. Sugar contributes to obesity.
23. High intake of sugar increases the risk of Crohn's disease and ulcerative colitis.
24. Sugar can cause changes frequently found in person with gastric or duodenal ulcers.
25. Sugar can cause arthritis.
26. Sugar can cause asthma.
27. Sugar can cause *Candida Albicans* (yeast infections).
28. Sugar can cause gallstones.
29. Sugar can cause ischemic heart disease.
30. Sugar can cause appendicitis.
31. Sugar can cause multiple sclerosis.
32. Sugar can cause hemorrhoids.
33. Sugar can cause varicose veins.
34. Sugar can elevate glucose and insulin responses in oral contraceptive users.
35. Sugar can lead to periodontal disease.
36. Sugar can contribute to osteoporosis.
37. Sugar contributes to saliva acidity.
38. Sugar can cause a decrease in insulin sensitivity.

39. Sugar leads to decreased glucose tolerance.
40. Sugar can decrease growth hormone.
41. Sugar can increase cholesterol.
42. Sugar can increase the systolic blood pressure.
43. Sugar can cause drowsiness and decreased activity in children.
44. Sugar can cause migraine headaches.
45. Sugar can interfere with the absorption of protein.
46. Sugar causes food allergies.
47. Sugar can contribute to diabetes.
48. Sugar can cause toxemia during pregnancy.
49. Sugar can contribute to eczema in children.
50. Sugar can cause cardiovascular disease.
51. Sugar can impair the structure of DNA.
52. Sugar can change the structure of protein.
53. Sugar can make our skin age by changing the structure of collagen.
54. Sugar can cause cataracts.
55. Sugar can cause atherosclerosis.
56. Sugar can cause emphysema.
57. Sugar can promote an elevation of low-density proteins (LDL).
58. Sugar can cause free radicals in the bloodstream.
59. Sugar lowers the enzymes' ability to function.
60. Sugar can cause loss of tissue elasticity and function.
61. Sugar can cause a permanent altering in the way the proteins act in the body.
62. Sugar can increase the size of the liver by making the liver cells divide.
63. Sugar can increase the amount of liver fat.

64. Sugar can increase kidney size and produce pathological changes in the kidney.
65. Sugar can damage the pancreas.
66. Sugar can increase the body's fluid retention.
67. Sugar is enemy number one of the bowel movement.
68. Sugar can cause myopia (nearsightedness).
69. Sugar can compromise the lining of the capillaries.
70. Sugar can make the tendons more brittle.
71. Sugar can cause headaches.
72. Sugar can overstress the pancreas.
73. Sugar can adversely affect school children's grades.
74. Sugar can cause an increase in delta, alpha and theta brain waves.
75. Sugar can cause depression.
76. Sugar increases the risk of gastric cancer.
77. Sugar can be a risk factor of gallbladder cancer.
78. Sugar can cause dyspepsia (indigestion).
79. Sugar can increase your risk of getting gout.
80. The ingestion of sugar can increase the levels of glucose in an oral glucose tolerance test over the ingestion of complex carbohydrates.
81. Sugar can increase the insulin responses in humans consuming high-sugar diets compared to low-sugar diets.
82. Sugar increases bacterial fermentation in the colon.
83. Sugar increases the risk of colon cancer in women.
84. There is a greater risk for Crohn's disease with people who have a high intake of sugar.
85. Sugar can cause platelet adhesiveness.
86. Sugar can cause hormonal imbalance.
87. Sugar can lead to the formation of kidney stones.

Appendix IV

Daily Program

Breakfast	Lunch	Dinner	Metabolic
_____	_____	_____	_____
_____	_____	_____	_____
_____	_____	_____	_____
_____	_____	_____	_____
_____	_____	_____	_____

Checklist   Plans for the Day

_____ Followed Food Plan
_____ Attended Meetings
_____ Exercised _____ Minutes
_____ Phone Calls
_____ Drank Water
_____ Meditation
_____ Prayer
_____ Literature
_____ Vitamins

Journal for Today

Appendix V

Daily Tenth-Step Checklist

This checklist includes an inventory of program strengths and weaknesses. Recognition of these helps us to avoid falling into destructive patterns. Add your own specific relapse warning signs, barriers to recovery and necessary recovery tools to develop your personalized daily inventory checklist.

- Weekly home meeting
- Additional meetings _____ times weekly
- Food plan/abstinence: plan, report, commit; weigh and measure
- Sponsor contact
- Literature
- Journal
- Gratitude list
- Step-Ten checklist
- Telephone contacts
- Pray daily
- Weigh once a month maximum
- Exercise forty-five minutes maximum, plus warm-up
- Service
- Ask for help

Check on these:

- Overwork
- Ego problems
- Fatigue
- Compulsive behavior
- HALTS (Did I get too Hungry, Angry, Lonely, Tired, Stressed?)
- Making time for me
- Depression
- Late for meetings
- Judging, criticizing and blaming others
- Unnecessary spending
- Dangerous people and places
- Compulsive eating
- Spontaneous eating
- Volume bingeing
- Undereating
- Overeating
- Eating trigger food
- Addictive eating of sugar, flour, wheat

Bibliography

Alcoholics Anonymous. *Alcoholics Anonymous (Third Edition)*. New York: Alcoholics Anonymous World Services, Inc., 1976.

Alcoholics Anonymous. *Dr. Bob and the Good Oldtimers*. New York: Alcoholics Anonymous World Services, Inc., 1980.

Alcoholics Anonymous. *Twelve Steps and Twelve Traditions*. New York: Alcoholics Anonymous World Services, Inc., 1981.

American Psychiatric Association. *Diagnostic and Statistical Manual of Mental Disorders, Fourth Edition*. Washington, DC: American Psychiatric Association, 1994.

Appleton, N. *Lick the Sugar Habit*. New York: Avery Publications, 1996.

Birketvedt, G., et al. "Behavioral and Neuroendocrine Characteristics of the Night-Eating Syndrome," *Journal of the American Medical Association*, 1999. Vol. 282, No. 7, 657–663.

Collins, K. *Are you dehydrated?* MSNBC Nutrition notes on the danger of not drinking enough fluids, April 1999.

Cousins, N. *The Biology of Hope and the Healing Power of the Human Spirit*. New York: Penguin, 1989.

Egger, J. "Food Allergy and the Central Nervous System" in *Food Allergy,* edited by D. Reinhardt and E. Schmidt. New York: Raven, 1988.

Food Addicts Anonymous. *Steps to Recovery.* West Palm Beach, FL: Food Addicts Anonymous, 1997.

Gislason, S. J. *Addictive Foods: Ingredients and Mechanisms. www.alphanutrition.com/eatingdisorders/addictivefoods.htm.* 1999.

Glass Half Empty? Dateline NBC report on the latest survey about American water drinking habits, June 1999.

Hayden, R. *How to Turn Your Money Life Around: The Money Book for Women.* Deerfield Beach, FL: Health Communications, Inc., 1992.

Keene, M. *Chocolate Is My Kryptonite.* Litchfield, Arizona: Saguaro Publishing, 1997.

Mokdad, et al. "The Spread of the Obesity Epidemic in the United States, 1991–1998," *Journal of the American Medical Association,* 1999. Vol. 282, No. 16, 1519–1522.

Noble, et al. "D2 Dopamine Receptor Gene and Obesity," *International Journal of Eating Disorders,* 1994. Vol. 15, No. 3, 205–217. New York: John Wiley & Sons, Inc.

Overeaters Anonymous. *The Twelve Steps and Twelve Traditions of Overeaters Anonymous.* Torrance, CA: Overeaters Anonymous, Inc., 1993.

Radcliffe, M. J. "Diagnostic Use of Dietary Regimes," in *Food Allergy and Intolerance,* edited by J. Brostoff and S. J. Challacombe. London: Bailliere Tindall, 1987.

Sheppard, K. *Food Addiction: The Body Knows,* rev. ed. Deerfield Beach, FL: Health Communications, Inc., 1993.

Wadley, G. "A Review of Exorphin Research," *Australasian Society for Human Biology News,* July 1994. 6(1), 6–8.

Wadley, G., and A. Martin. "The Origins of Agriculture–A Biological Perspective and a New Hypothesis," *Australian Biologist,* June 1993. 6: 96–105.

About the Author

Kay Sheppard, M.A., a recovering food addict, is the best-selling author of *Food Addiction: The Body Knows.* She is a licensed mental health counselor and a certified eating disorders specialist. An internationally known consultant, trainer and therapist, she conducts intensive five-day stabilization and weekend workshops for food addicts in the United States, Canada, Mexico, Iceland, Germany and Denmark. She has worked with clients from all fifty states. Kay is a charter member of the International Association of Eating Disorders Professionals.

Since its publication, *Food Addiction: The Body Knows,* has become a primary resource for food addicts, bulimics and compulsive eaters. It is currently on the conference-approved literature list of two Twelve Step programs for food addicts. This book stands alone as a model for recovery from addiction to food substances.

Currently, Kay hosts the food addiction conference for America Online's Addictions and Recovery Forum. She manages a message board and handles hundreds of e-mails every week from food addicts looking for solutions.

Kay's personal recovery began in 1967. She lives on the Florida Space Coast.

Contact her at e-mail: *KShepp825@aol.com.*

Also from Kay Sheppard
Food Addiction: The Body Knows

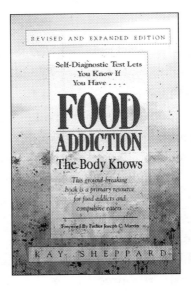

Code #276X • Quality Paperback • $9.95

This bestselling volume on food addiction has become a primary resource for food addicts and compulsive eaters. Here food addiction is defined, trigger foods are identified and consequences of food addiction are revealed. A lifetime eating plan demonstrating how to stick with a healthful food plan for the long term is also provided.